Early Praise for *Numerical Brain Teasers*

Enhance your numerical skills while enjoying pitting your wits against deceptively simple puzzles. I like the short descriptions of how the puzzles arose, and occasional hints of deeper mathematics lurking just below the surface. Engaging, attractive, and tremendous fun. Educational, too!

➤ **Ian Stewart**
Emeritus Professor of Mathematics, University of Warwick

These were fun to solve one by one, but the real fun was in writing solvers for each class of problem.

➤ **Ricardo Signes**
CTO, Fastmail

A delicious way of wasting time—which makes it not a waste at all.

➤ **Jon Skeet**
International Author and Speaker

I was skeptical at first, but this book really has my number.

➤ **Jill Rouleau**
Ansible Cloud Architect

Thirty seconds after opening this book I was scribbling on a scratch pad to work on these "crunchy" puzzles. Irresistible!

➤ **Mike Pope**
Technical Writer and Editor

This is a wonderful collection of math puzzles, some traditional, others new. There's plenty here to challenge the most seasoned puzzle solver.

➤ **Walt Mankowski**
Senior Data Analyst, University of Pennsylvania

Numerical Brain Teasers

Exercise Your Mind

Erica Sadun

The Pragmatic Bookshelf

Raleigh, North Carolina

For our complete catalog of hands-on, practical, and Pragmatic content for software developers, please visit *https://pragprog.com*.

The team that produced this book includes:

CEO: Dave Rankin
COO: Janet Furlow
Managing Editor: Tammy Coron
Development Editor: Brian MacDonald
Copy Editor: L. Sakhi MacMillan
Indexing: Potomac Indexing, LLC
Layout: Gilson Graphics
Founders: Andy Hunt and Dave Thomas

For sales, volume licensing, and support, please contact *support@pragprog.com*.

For international rights, please contact *rights@pragprog.com*.

ISBN-13: 978-1-68050-974-8
Book version: P1.0—January 2023

Contents

Part I — Brain Teasers

Acknowledgments

Thank you to all the subscribers of the @pragprog Twitter account who made this book possible by viewing, liking, and interacting with my puzzle tweets. It's been so much fun creating and sharing these brain teasers with you and I'm grateful to have an audience that's as excited about them as I am.

Thank you, as well, to my development editor, Brian MacDonald, who knows the difference between Spidermen and Spider-Men and is willing to put up with my quirky authorship.

Thank you to my technical reviewers, who graciously put in the time working through my puzzles, my logic, and my storytelling to make sure I was as accurate as possible. All mistakes are my own. Many of my correct statements are due to them. Specifically, thank you to Frances Buontempo, Trevor Burnham, Zulfikar Dharmawan, Michael Fazio, Derek Graham, Andy Lester, Daivid Morgan, Jason Pike, Karl Stolley, and Roman Zabicki.

Additional thanks to Dave Rankin, Pragmatic CEO, and the one who said, "Why don't you put those puzzle things all together in a book?" I did and that's why this book exists.

To my husband and children, I can only do this because you make it possible. Thank you all for being yourselves and enriching my life.

Introduction

I have always loved puzzles. From the time I was a child, my extended family surrounded me with them. They would put aside clippings from newspapers for us kids and indulge us with small books of collected puzzles. Recently, my dad was under the weather. I sent him a family care package: some snacks and a book of word-find puzzles.

There's something comforting about engaging the mind. Each solution brings diversion and, possibly, a dash of endorphins or some other brain chemical, helping lift you up as you conquer every challenge. They're a wonderful way to get your brain going when you're starting work, to divert you during a short break, or to help you transition back to normal life when your workday ends.

A good puzzle has a bit of crunch to it. It challenges, rewards, and then allows you to move on with life, having entertained yourself or learned something. Puzzles are momentary delights. My best-selling iOS apps were built around number-, word-, and logic-puzzles.

This book collects styles of number-based puzzles. It's full of quick brain-teasing games. It's a mix of puzzles and storytelling so I can share my delight of these numeric conundrums with you.

Each chapter is devoted to a different style. You'll find a mix of traditional and new puzzles, unified by their focus on arithmetic, geometry, and logic. These puzzles allow you to explore a style of math head-scratcher and then test out your skills on real challenges.

Thank you for reading this book. I'm so glad that I get to share these little joys with you.

About the Author

Erica Sadun enjoys deep diving into technology and has written, co-written, and contributed to dozens of books about computing and digital media. Sadun has blogged at TUAW, Ars Technica, O'Reilly, and Lifehacker. She's also dabbled extensively in programming, teaching, and developer outreach. She has spent years wandering through the halls of academia, collecting degrees in Math and Computer Science along the way. She has also raised several children. Sadun loves reading books as much as writing them.

About You

This book assumes you love playing with numbers and puzzles. Nothing more. *Numerical Brain Teasers* has been written to entertain and delight. You may learn a few things along the way, but the entire point of this book is to engage and divert you. I hope you have as much fun working through these puzzles as I did putting them together.

Part I

Brain Teasers

Number Combinations

3	6
5	5

23

How to Play

Solve this puzzle by combining 3, 6, 5, and 5 to produce 23. Use only basic math operators.

Keep these rules in mind:

- Use every digit exactly once in any order.

- You may only add, subtract, multiply, or divide.

- If you need to, add parentheses.

- Grade-school math only. You don't need logs, factorials, decimals, exponentiation, or any other fancy math functions.

- Don't rotate numbers. For example, a 9 is not a 6.

- Don't put digits together; 1 and 4 don't make 14.

- Programmers, remember that 3 divided by 2 is $1\frac{1}{2}$, not 1.

For more information about this puzzle and its solution, turn the page. When you're ready for more puzzles like this one, see Having Fun with More Puzzles, on page 8.

About This Puzzle

Here is my answer to the puzzle in math form: $5 \times 5 - 6 \div 3 = 23$. Does that match your answer? It may or may not. Any correct equation that gets you to the right target is okay. Read on to learn how I solved this puzzle.

Build a Solution

Do you like to mess with arithmetic? Number combinations are a perfect challenge. Given a set of numbers, can you combine them using only basic math operators? I love these puzzles; they're one of my favorites kinds to turn to.

For this sample puzzle, I used multiplication to get 25. That's because 25 is fairly close to 23, the goal number. It can help to get near the target first like this. Then, see if you can adjust with the remaining numbers. Next, I lowered the total by 2 to hit 23, my target value.

Move boldly and sometimes you can capture that easy win. "Getting close" is a great strategy for the many times this works. Don't get caught up in a multiply/divide-only mindset. Try to subtract and add each number from the target. See if a clear path pops out. When this approach works, it reframes the puzzle with fewer numbers.

Some number combination puzzles have only one or two ways to solve them. Others offer lots of solutions, like the following example. The challenge looks a bit like the previous sample but, as you'll see, there are many more ways to solve it.

9	6	
3	2	39

This puzzle has dozens of solutions. I think there are more than fifty correct ways to combine these numbers. Here are a few answers you might come up with:

$$(2 + 3) \times 6 + 9$$
$$3 \times (6 - 2 + 9)$$
$$3 + (6 - 2) \times 9$$
$$3 \times (6 - (2 - 9))$$
$$(3 \times (9 + 2)) + 6$$
$$3 \times 9 + 2 \times 6$$

Having so many possible answers doesn't make this puzzle any less fun. If anything, I love seeing if I can come up with "just one more" solution. Many answers means there are more ways to get there. These "loose" puzzles are great for groups, where people can keep adding new solutions. Yes, some puzzles only offer one solution. More often, you have several to work with. Even if you're flipping terms, there's usually more than one possible answer.

Is your target number divisible by 3? If so, see whether you can construct multiples of 3 by adding or subtracting pairs of numbers. This can help you find even more solutions!

Background

Parker Brothers published a number combination game called Krypto[1] in 1963. It uses a deck of fifty-six cards. In each round, the dealer places a target card and five number cards ranging from 1 to 25. Players combine the number cards to reach the target. Because the number cards go up to 25, and there are five cards to work with, rounds can be pretty challenging. Single digit puzzles, like the ones in this chapter, are much quicker to solve.

Another version of number combination was popular in 1960s Shanghai.[2] The target for each hand was always set at 24. Players use forty number cards from Ace (1) to 10, dealt out in stacks. Players pulled playing cards from their stack to set the puzzle. The first correct answer "won" the hand.

Using playing cards, make an easy-to-travel game. You can add dice like a D20 roleplaying die to create targets other than 24. Remember, there's not always a solution for every target and four-card set.

I first met combination puzzles in elementary school. They, or other puzzles, waited for us every day on the blackboard. These puzzles kept us students quiet and engaged first thing in the morning as our teacher got a break to get organized and moving.

Like the card game, my teachers always used four-digit puzzles. I believe they had some source of "busy activities," like worksheets or education books, that used this style. Over time, I've seen many variations. It's now common to see puzzles with three numbers at a time in math education. In newsletters and magazines, I've seen combination puzzles with as many as six or eight numbers at a time.

---

1. https://en.wikipedia.org/wiki/Krypto_(game)
2. https://www.pagat.com/adders/24.html

As you add extra terms, like in Krypto, you add complexity. I prefer fewer digits and a shorter solve time. Four seems like the perfect number to keep puzzles tight. It creates a quick, focused, fun style of brain teaser that usually takes less than a minute or two to solve.

Also, I limit my puzzles to single digits. There's just enough crunch to keep things interesting, without making them tedious. Brain teasers shouldn't feel like work. Well-designed puzzles, short or long, should be fun to solve and satisfying when finished.

Strategies

Puzzles with only addition and subtraction are the easiest to solve. Sum up the numbers and see if and how far you've overshot. More challenging puzzles use multiplication and division. Strategies help you attack those combinations.

One good strategy is to look for a target's factors. Factors are numbers that can easily divide another number. Looking for factors helps break the puzzle down into simpler problems. Try to create those factors without running out of digits.

Factors kept the "make 39 from 2, 3, 6 and 9" puzzle from the start of this chapter loose and flexible. The numbers 3 and 2 are factors of 9 and 6. Extra factors gives you more numbers through division. Those extra numbers can combine for more outcomes.

You can use up numbers by turning them into 1s or 0s. Then, when you're at your target, you can multiply/divide by 1, or add/subtract 0. For example, consider the numbers in this puzzle:

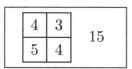

5 times 3 gets you right to the solution. So, what do you do with the extra 4s? If you transform them to 1 or 0, you can cut them from the puzzle: $(4 \div 4) \times 5 \times 3$.

Try using small values to add or subtract as you approach your target number. Check how close you can get and then use the remaining numbers to wiggle into place. That's what I did with the example at the start of the chapter.

Finally, as you solve more puzzles you'll start to recognize common patterns. Many of the challenges resemble each other in the way you solve them. Do you worry they'll get boring? I've played with these puzzles for decades. They're still a delight for me. I hope you like them too.

Having Fun with More Puzzles

Now that you've seen what a combination puzzle looks like and learned the rules, it's time to dive in and try out some puzzles on your own. An answer key follows the puzzles.

Puzzle 1

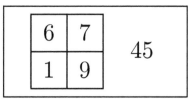

Puzzle 2

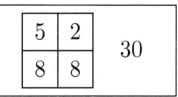

Puzzle 3

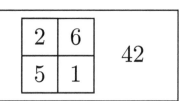

Puzzle 4

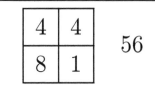

Puzzle 5

6	1
1	4

5

Puzzle 6

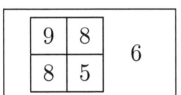

6

Puzzle 7

4	3
4	7

45

Puzzle 8

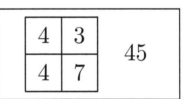

60

Puzzle 9

7	7
5	4

51

Puzzle 10

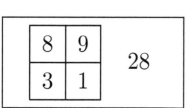

8	9
3	1

28

Puzzle 11

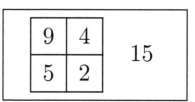

9	4
5	2

15

Puzzle 12

2	5
7	8

39

Puzzle 13

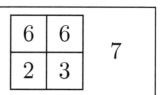

6	6
2	3

7

Puzzle 14

4	2
4	5

24

Puzzle 15

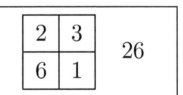

Puzzle 16

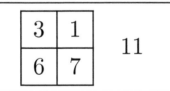

Puzzle 17

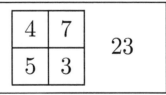

Puzzle 18

Puzzle 19

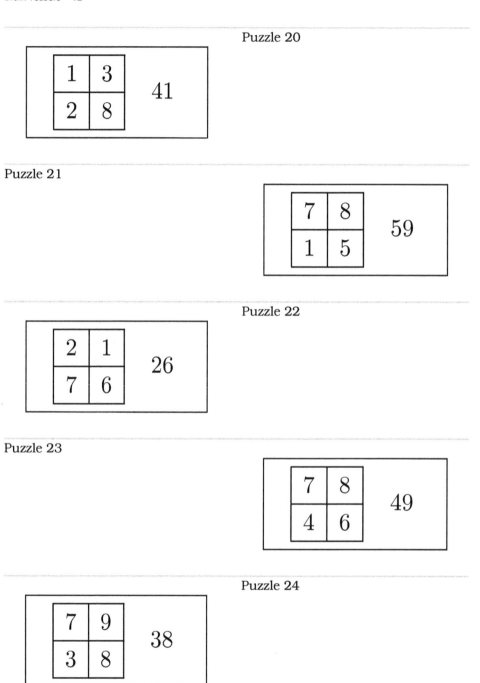

Puzzle 20

1	3
2	8

41

Puzzle 21

7	8
1	5

59

Puzzle 22

2	1
7	6

26

Puzzle 23

7	8
4	6

49

Puzzle 24

7	9
3	8

38

Puzzle 25

Puzzle 26

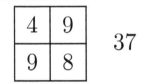

Puzzle 27

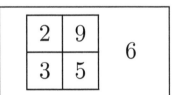

Puzzle 28

Puzzle 29

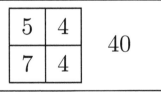

8	9
2	8

39

Solutions

Here's a solution for every puzzle. Remember: most solutions are not unique. That's part of the fun and the joy of combination puzzles. Your correct answer may be different from the ones I include in the following key.

Puzzle 1	$9 + (7 - 1) \times 6 = 45$
Puzzle 2	$5 \times 8 - (8 + 2) = 30$
Puzzle 3	$(5 + 2) \times 6 \times 1 = 42$
Puzzle 4	$(4 + 4) \times (8 - 1) = 56$
Puzzle 5	$(6 + 4) \div (1 + 1) = 5$
Puzzle 6	$8 - 8 \div (9 - 5) = 6$
Puzzle 7	$3 \times (7 + 4 + 4) = 45$
Puzzle 8	$(8 + 2) \times 3 \times 2 = 60$
Puzzle 9	$(7 + 7) \times 4 - 5 = 51$
Puzzle 10	$(3 + 1) \times 9 - 8 = 28$
Puzzle 11	$2 \times (9 - 4) + 5 = 15$
Puzzle 12	$7 \times 5 + 8 \div 2 = 39$
Puzzle 13	$2 \times 3 + 6 \div 6 = 7$
Puzzle 14	$(2 + 5) \times 4 - 4 = 24$
Puzzle 15	$8 + (6 - 6) \div 3 = 8$
Puzzle 16	$7 + 4 \times 9 \div 3 = 19$
Puzzle 17	$6 \times (1 + 3) + 2 = 26$
Puzzle 18	$7 + 6 + 1 - 3 = 11$
Puzzle 19	$7 \times 5 - 3 \times 4 = 23$
Puzzle 20	$(2 + 3) \times 8 + 1 = 41$
Puzzle 21	$8 \times (7 + 1) - 5 = 59$
Puzzle 22	$1 \times (6 + 7) \times 2 = 26$
Puzzle 23	$(8 + 6) \times 4 - 7 = 49$
Puzzle 24	$7 \times 3 + 9 + 8 = 38$
Puzzle 25	$4 \times (6 + 3 - 1) = 32$
Puzzle 26	$4 \times (7 + 2) + 6 = 42$
Puzzle 27	$3 \times (9 - 5) \div 2 = 6$
Puzzle 28	$9 \times (9 - 4) - 8 = 37$
Puzzle 29	$5 \times (7 + 4 \div 4) = 40$
Puzzle 30	$(8 - 2) \times 8 - 9 = 39$

Summing Grids

2				12
		6	2	12
5	1			13
3	5			15
4				17
6	2	3		15

How to Play

Add the digits 1 through 6 to every white column. The grey column on the right holds the sum of each row. Fill empty cells so the sums are correct and every digit from 1 to 6 appears in each white column.

Keep these rules in mind:

- Each digit must appear exactly once in each of the white columns.

- The sum for each row must be correct.

- Numbers may repeat across rows. A single row might contain, for example, a pair of 2s or 5s—or no repeats at all.

For more information about this puzzle and its solution, turn the page. When you're ready for more puzzles like this one, see Having Fun with More Puzzles, on page 22.

About This Puzzle

Summing puzzles offer a quick challenge built on sums and a little logic. Each puzzle is a 2D grid. The grid contains a mix of blanks and numbers, with a special column on its right. You fill in any empty spaces with the missing number that belongs there.

Summing grid puzzles involve math and logic. Start by looking for easy wins. If any row or column is missing only one value, fill it in right away. For rows, sum up the numbers that appear and subtract that from the total. For columns, figure out which digit is missing and fill that in. Keep pushing forward with the new information until you exhaust the easy wins.

2				12
1	**3**	6	2	12
5	1			13
3	5			15
4				17
6	2	3	**4**	15

In this puzzle, there's a single empty square in both the first column and the final row. The first column number must be 1. 1 is the only digit left between 1 and 6 in column one. Subtracting 11, the sum of row six from 15 leaves 4.

Easy wins may or may not exist in any given puzzle. They depend on layout, size, and difficulty. More rows and columns can mean more empty spaces. The number of clues affects how hard a puzzle is.

Solving column one opens up row two, which then has just a single space left. As the sum of 1, 6, and 2 is 9, and the row sum is 12, the remaining digit in that row must be 3.

Next, consider each column's remaining digits. You always know the unused numbers for any column. If you're working on paper, write each column's missing numbers above or into the column's first box. You can erase or cross them out later. On a computer or tablet, use a stylus or drawing program. This often allows you to move those numbers around later; very handy!

2	$\frac{4\,6}{}$	$\frac{1\,4}{2\,5}$	$\frac{3\,1}{6\,5}$	12
1	**3**	6	2	12
5	1			13
3	5			15
4				17
6	2	3	**4**	15

For this example, two choices remain for the second column in the first and fifth rows: 4 and 6. The fifth row's sum is high (17). Try picking the larger digit for this row. This doesn't always work out but it's a sound approach.

Now, look for rows with only two numbers missing. Both rows three and four need a count of 7 to reach their target sums. (And so does row five, if that 6 is right.) Consider how this count might break down. You can make 7 from 1 and 6, 2 and 5, or 3 and 4.

Use this information to lay out your numbers. Make a rough approximation and try to keep your sums in mind. This grows difficult when you have more squares to work on. You'll need to consider more ways that digits sum together.

2	**4**	**5**	**3**	⑫
1	**3**	6	2	12
5	1	**4**	**1**	⑬
3	5	**1**	**6**	15
4	**6**	**2**	**5**	17
6	2	3	**4**	15

With your rough solution laid out, calculate your sums and note any rows that are incorrect. The two circles show rows with wrong sums. In both cases, the sums are off by 2.

2	**4**	**5**	**<u>1</u>**	12
1	**3**	6	2	12
5	1	**4**	**<u>3</u>**	13
3	5	**1**	**6**	15
4	**6**	**2**	**5**	17
6	2	3	**4**	15

You can flip two pairs: 5 and 4 in column three, and 3 and 1 in column four. Of these, only 3 and 1 are different by 2. Swapping the 3 and the 1 completes and solves this puzzle. In the completed puzzle, the digits in every row correspond to the sum on the right and every column contains the digits 1 through 6.

These strategies of easy wins, reduced sums, count breakdowns, and rough approximations should help you through all but the most difficult puzzles.

Background

Summing grids are a popular challenge. Variations include vertical layout with sums on the side, like here, and horizontal, with sums at the bottom. I've seen puzzles with as few as three or four sets of numbers and as many as seven or eight. More sets increases each puzzle's challenge. Solving them is a little messier.

In the preceding sample, I used six digits (1 through 6) per set. The largest puzzles may use nine or ten numbers for each set. The most famous style of summing grids I've found is the Zehnergitter, also called Tenner Grid puzzles and Grid Ten. They're commonly used in math education as well as for recreation.

These puzzles use the digits 0 through 9 laid out in rows with sums at the bottom. Some variations use the first ten numbers rather than single digits. Puzzles that target young solvers often add more clues. This reduces frustration and creates an easier path toward victory.

Here's an example for you to try. I've placed a solution for it into this chapter's answer key. The strategies and approach are the same as any other summing grid puzzle.

Complete the Grid

Use the digits 0–9 to complete each white row. The sums of each column add to the values in the grey row.

2	4		7			6			0
	5	7	0		6	4		2	9
3	5	7				4	2		
7	9	1			6		0	2	5
20	23	20	15	15	26	17	8	14	22

Having Fun with More Puzzles

Now that you've seen samples and read about strategy, try some more. Enjoy the summing grid puzzles on the next few pages. An answer key follows the puzzles.

Puzzle 1

5	1	2		11
			1	16
		3		12
2		6	4	17
		1	2	10
			5	18

Puzzle 2

4			2	12
6	2			12
	6	2		12
1		6	5	16
	5			14
	3			18

Puzzle 3

6	2		5	16
5	1		4	12
				14
			3	12
4			1	16
		4	6	14

Puzzle 4

				18
1				13
2		1	4	13
6	1		2	13
5			3	16
3	5			11

Puzzle 5

		2		11
			5	12
	1	5		15
1		6	4	16
3	6		2	15
	4			15

Puzzle 6

3		6		14
		1	4	12
			5	16
4	1	5		12
				18
1	3	2		12

Puzzle 7

1			6	15
2	4	1		12
5	3		2	14
	1			14
	2		4	17
				12

Puzzle 8

	3		5	14
		3		14
3	1		4	14
1	6		3	15
		1	6	14
				13

Puzzle 9

3	5	7		2	4	22
2	8		4	7	5	29
1		4	6	8	7	29
8					1	24
6			2	1		21
		8	7		2	29
7	6			3		30
					6	32

Puzzle 10

	1		2	9		28
	5	4	7		1	27
2		5		4		29
1		3	8		4	27
	2	1				31
4	7	2	5	6		33
7		9	1	3	2	26
3		8	4	1		31
		6		7	8	38

Puzzle 11

		1		3	4	9			
3	1	9	7	0	4	8	6	2	
1		8		2	4	3	9		0
	1		3					5	6
12	16	26	17	9	12	27	32	18	11

Puzzle 12

	4		1		5		8		6
		4		2			0	8	5
6	2	0	9	8	1		5	4	7
7				1	3	0	8		
24	9	16	23	18	12	9	21	25	23

Puzzle 13

	0	7				5			8
	8		0	9	1	5	6		
	3	0	1	2	8	9		6	
			6	8	7	5	0	2	1
20	14	18	11	22	22	24	11	20	18

Puzzle 14

1		9	8	4	3			6	
	9			0	6	2	3		4
7		4			8	3	9	0	5
		7	4	8		6		1	
16	22	21	19	18	20	11	19	14	20

Puzzle 15

7	2		3		4	5	9		
4			5	1	6	8	3		
	2			7		8	5	1	4
4		2				7	5	3	0
18	14	9	23	22	25	28	22	12	7

Solutions

Summing-grid puzzle solutions are not always unique. Your answers may vary from the ones provided. Sometimes two pairs of numbers in four grid cells are interchangeable.

Here's the solution to the Zehnergitter found within the chapter:

2	4	5	7	1	8	6	3	9	0
8	5	7	0	1	6	4	3	2	9
3	5	7	0	9	6	4	2	1	8
7	9	1	8	4	6	3	0	2	5
20	23	20	15	15	26	17	8	14	22

Puzzle 1

5	1	2	3	11
4	6	5	1	16
1	2	3	6	12
2	5	6	4	17
3	4	1	2	10
6	3	4	5	18

Puzzle 2

4	1	5	2	12
6	2	1	3	12
3	6	2	1	12
1	4	6	5	16
2	5	3	4	14
5	3	4	6	18

Puzzle 3

6	2	3	5	16
5	1	2	4	12
3	4	5	2	14
2	6	1	3	12
4	5	6	1	16
1	3	4	6	14

Puzzle 4

4	3	5	6	18
1	4	3	5	13
2	6	1	4	13
6	1	4	2	13
5	2	6	3	16
3	5	2	1	11

Puzzle 5

5	3	2	1	11
4	2	1	5	12
6	1	5	3	15
1	5	6	4	16
3	6	4	2	15
2	4	3	6	15

Puzzle 6

3	4	6	1	14
2	5	1	4	12
6	2	3	5	16
4	1	5	2	12
5	6	4	3	18
1	3	2	6	12

Puzzle 7

1	5	3	6	15
2	4	1	5	12
5	3	4	2	14
4	1	6	3	14
6	2	5	4	17
3	6	2	1	12

Puzzle 8

4	3	2	5	14
5	4	3	2	14
3	1	6	4	14
1	6	5	3	15
2	5	1	6	14
6	2	4	1	13

Puzzle 9

3	5	7	1	2	4	22
2	8	3	4	7	5	29
1	3	4	6	8	7	29
8	2	6	3	4	1	24
6	4	5	2	1	3	21
5	1	8	7	6	2	29
7	6	1	5	3	8	30
4	7	2	8	5	6	32

Puzzle 10

6	1	7	2	9	3	28
8	5	4	7	2	1	27
2	8	5	3	4	7	29
1	6	3	8	5	4	27
9	2	1	6	8	5	31
4	7	2	5	6	9	33
7	4	9	1	3	2	26
3	9	8	4	1	6	31
5	3	6	9	7	8	38

Puzzle 11

6	7	1	2	3	4	9	8	5	0
3	1	9	7	0	4	8	6	2	5
1	7	8	5	2	4	3	9	6	0
2	1	8	3	4	0	7	9	5	6
12	16	26	17	9	12	27	32	18	11

Puzzle 12

2	4	3	1	7	5	0	8	9	6
9	1	4	7	2	3	6	0	8	5
6	2	0	9	8	1	3	5	4	7
7	2	9	6	1	3	0	8	4	5
24	9	16	23	18	12	9	21	25	23

Puzzle 13

2	0	7	4	3	6	5	1	9	8
4	8	7	0	9	1	5	6	3	2
5	3	0	1	2	8	9	4	6	7
9	3	4	6	8	7	5	0	2	1
20	14	18	11	22	22	24	11	20	18

Puzzle 14

1	7	9	8	4	3	0	5	6	2
8	9	1	5	0	6	2	3	7	4
7	1	4	2	6	8	3	9	0	5
0	5	7	4	8	3	6	2	1	9
16	22	21	19	18	20	11	19	14	20

Puzzle 15

7	2	0	3	6	4	5	9	8	1
4	9	7	5	1	6	8	3	0	2
3	2	0	9	7	6	8	5	1	4
4	1	2	6	8	9	7	5	3	0
18	14	9	23	22	25	28	22	12	7

Wandering Digits

$$5920 + 894 = 146614$$

How to Play

 A digit has wandered from its normal location, perhaps intending a life of adventure. Now it is in the wrong place in the equation. It is sad and lost, the equation broken. Help identify and return it home to correct the equation and make the digit happy again.

For more information about this puzzle and its solution, turn the page. When you're ready for more puzzles like this one, see Having Fun with More Puzzles, on page 36.

About This Puzzle

Imagine, if you will, a number with restless digits. Sometimes one will wander from its place in an equation and settle somewhere new. That's fodder for a quick and fun little puzzle.

Consider the example puzzle. The weird sum tells you something has gone wrong. You'd expect to see a sum closer to 6,000 than 146,000 in this equation. What's happened, of course, is a wandering digit. One of these digits has strayed from its correct location and sat itself somewhere else.

So what broke? Is an answer immediately obvious? It's up to you to save the day, solve the equation, and move the wandering digit back home where it belongs.

Solving the Example

In this example, the second digit of the second term, a 6, has moved a term to the right. Returning it fixes the equation.

$$5920 + 894 = 146614$$

$$5920 + 8694 = 14614$$

With these puzzles, start working from right to left. As long as the sums and the digits remain correct, omit them from consideration. For example, the final digits are 0 plus 4. That adds to 4. Correct. Next, 2 plus 9 is 11. Also correct, with a carry of 1.

$$5920 + 894 = 146614$$

Continuing, 9 plus 8 is 17. With 1 carried, that adds to 18. That partial sum definitely does not end in 6, even if you squint. Based on its size, the second term has most likely lost a digit. This is where you should consider inserting the current digit from the six-digit sum. Third from the right feels correct.

$$5920 + 894 = 146614$$

Moving that 6 from the sum to the second term changes the current equation from 9 plus 8 to 9 plus 6, or 15. Add in the carry and you get 16, a match. With this, the puzzle is solved.

$$5920 + 894 = 146614$$

Wandering digit puzzles grow harder when the digit count doesn't change. In this sample, you could tell from the size that a digit would move to the second term. When digit counts don't change, use right-to-left math and compare to the sum or difference. Deciding which digit to move becomes a tiny bit trickier. Hopefully, the puzzle is still just as much fun.

Following the page break, you'll find puzzles to work on. An answer key follows the puzzles.

Having Fun with More Puzzles

Puzzle 1	Puzzle 2
$716 - 5903 = 16263$	$3863 - 3633 = -2470$

Puzzle 3	Puzzle 4
$65408 + 2523 = 971$	$7440 + 2869 = 7339$

Puzzle 5	Puzzle 6
$490 - 37264 = -1274$	$356 + 6706 = 101462$

Puzzle 7

358 + 73933 = 11471

Puzzle 8

57442 + 4129 = 1171

Puzzle 9

862 + 3875 = 142517

Puzzle 10

3568 − 57745 = −217

Puzzle 11

3735 − 386 = −7141

Puzzle 12

5893 − 901 = 9942

Puzzle 13

22059 − 89755 = −76696

Puzzle 14

39324 + 35375 = 72899

Puzzle 15

11505 − 43875 = −62880

Puzzle 16

69411 + 8787 = 6138198

Puzzle 17

636611 − 52115 = 1149

Puzzle 18

234760 + 145964 = 419424

Puzzle 19

770064 − 491942 = 278698

Puzzle 20

280004 − 402466 = −212462

Puzzle 21

115991 − 421052 = −301461

Puzzle 22

136901 + 140476 = 277737

Puzzle 23

41111 − 74464 = 3367077

Puzzle 24

79685 − 368592 = 4123093

Solutions

Puzzle 1	$7166 - 5903 = 1263$
Puzzle 2	$3863 - 6333 = -2470$
Puzzle 3	$6548 + 2523 = 9071$
Puzzle 4	$4470 + 2869 = 7339$
Puzzle 5	$2490 - 3764 = -1274$
Puzzle 6	$3456 + 6706 = 10162$
Puzzle 7	$3538 + 7933 = 11471$
Puzzle 8	$7442 + 4129 = 11571$
Puzzle 9	$8642 + 3875 = 12517$
Puzzle 10	$3568 - 5745 = -2177$
Puzzle 11	$3735 - 3876 = -141$
Puzzle 12	$5893 - 4901 = 992$
Puzzle 13	$22059 - 89755 = -67696$
Puzzle 14	$39324 + 33575 = 72899$
Puzzle 15	$11505 - 74385 = -62880$
Puzzle 16	$69411 + 68787 = 138198$
Puzzle 17	$63611 - 52115 = 11496$
Puzzle 18	$273460 + 145964 = 419424$
Puzzle 19	$770640 - 491942 = 278698$
Puzzle 20	$280004 - 402466 = -122462$
Puzzle 21	$119591 - 421052 = -301461$
Puzzle 22	$136901 + 140476 = 277377$
Puzzle 23	$411171 - 74464 = 336707$
Puzzle 24	$791685 - 368592 = 423093$

Skips

	4		1	1	3	
		2	1	–		3
2		–	3	1		
	–	1	4			2
3	3	4			1	1
1		3	2		–	
	1		2			

How to Play

Place the numbers 1 through 4 into the white puzzle grid. A number may appear only once in any given row or column. The gray border surrounding the grid contains hints. A hint shows the nearest number along its row or column. But there's a twist. A *skip*, written as a dash (–), lets the hint pass through a box and continue to the next number. In this puzzle, one skip appears in each row and column.

For more information about this puzzle and its solution, turn the page. When you're ready for more puzzles like this one, see Having Fun with More Puzzles, on page 46.

About This Puzzle

Skips are marvelous puzzles that live in the Sudoku family. Like Sudoku, only one of each number may appear in a row or column. Yet, skip puzzles are simpler than Sudoku and easier to solve. They use fewer numbers and around each game board are hints, helping you fill cells. They also have a wonderful twist of *skipping*.

In the game, you're given a range of numbers, for example 1 through 5, and a board. Each puzzle also includes one or more skips, shown as dashes (–). Skips follow the same restrictions as numbers. If a puzzle uses two skips, every column and row contains exactly two skips.

Here's a typical puzzle. This board uses the numbers 1–3 plus two skips for each row and column. Some numbers and skips are pre-filled. I call these *clues*. They narrow the options for the rows and columns around them. Gray *hints* appear around the side. The hints tell you facts about nearby numbers. You solve the board by completing the empty squares.

◇			1	3		◇
	3		1		–	
2	–	–	2	3		
	2	3		1		
	1	–	3	–		
	–		–	2		
◇		1	3		3	◇

This is the same puzzle with the board solved. I filled all the hints around the grey edges to show how this unusual puzzle feature works.

◇	3	2	1	3	1	◇
3	3	2	1	–	–	1
2	–	–	2	3	1	1
2	2	3	–	1	–	1
1	1	–	3	–	2	2
1	–	1	–	2	3	3
◇	1	1	3	2	3	◇

In skip puzzles, hints describe the nearest number along a column or row. "Nearest" doesn't always mean the closest square. That's because hints pass through skip (–) squares to reach the first number. This gives the puzzle more challenge because hints don't just tell you the answer. They provide a direction and a value but nothing more.

It's up to you to figure out if the nearest number is right next to the hint or separated by one or more skips. For example, the hints on the left for both the second and third rows are 2. On the second row, 2 is in the third column, on the third row in the first. The second row hint skips twice before reaching a number. Look around the board. You'll see examples without skips, with one skip, and double skips, like that 2 on the second row.

Skipping forms the heart of this puzzle. It's what makes them so much fun. You can't always be sure exactly where that hint lands. So use your brain to figure it out! Like the clues scattered on the central grid, hints give you a direction to start thinking.

Solving the Example

Here's the answer to the puzzle, and a walk-through explaining the steps to reach that answer. After working through the puzzle, you may notice that there was no ambiguity. This was intentional. Not all skip puzzles are so clear. As they get larger with fewer hints and clues, the challenge grows as well.

◇	4	**2**	1	1	3	◇
4	**4**	2	1	–	**3**	3
2	**2**	–	3	1	**4**	**4**
1	–	1	4	**3**	**2**	2
3	3	4	∸	**2**	1	1
1	**1**	3	2	**4**	–	**4**
◇	1	**3**	2	**4**	**1**	◇

Finding the Solution

Start your solve by searching for the easiest answers. An easy value is one you can solve without ambiguity. The hints and clues on the board help guide you. They limit the possibilities for other squares, so you can directly deduce values. After finishing the easy wins, use logic to reason your way through any remaining squares.

Here's how I worked through this puzzle:

- Row two starts with a blank and a skip. The hint says 2, so the first number must also be 2. Puzzles with more than one skip won't be this straightforward.

- Placing that 2 means the number above it must be a 4. This information is from the top column-one hint.

- Both rows now have four items filled. Eliminating those from the set of (1, 2, 3, 4, –) leaves only one possibility. The only number left for row one must be 3, and for row two, 4. Enter the values into column five.

- You don't have to, but I fill in hints as well as grid numbers. It feels cleaner and more complete. Row one's left hint is 4 and row three's is 1. Row two's right hint is 4.

- Row five's first number must be 1. Two hints and those 3s offer no other choice.

- That leaves 4 for row five, column four, as the remaining option. If you're filling hints, add those as well.

- There's now enough information to complete the hints in the bottom row: 1, 3, 2, 4, 1.

- Look at column five. All the values are there except for row three. Enter the 2.

- Complete row four. The numbers 1 through 4 are already in use, so the missing value is a skip (–) in column three.

- Finish the puzzle by adding the 3 to row three/column four.

With that, you've completed the puzzle. This puzzle demonstrated the use of hints, clues, and skips. Many skip puzzles are more challenging. They have fewer clues, and their solutions are not always unique.

Background

I first found the "hint and skip" notion in a puzzle from one of my daughter's video games. Over time, I've occasionally seen seen similar puzzles online. They use small boards and a single skip. When designing puzzles for my own use, I find I prefer much larger boards, such as 8×8 grids. I came up with extra skips to add another layer of challenge. The puzzles I write for myself tend to be big and messy.

Skip puzzles are one of my favorite time-wasters. This book contains a mix of quick puzzles and longer games. These fall more into the latter category. In choosing which boards to include for this chapter, I decided to mix up some short and simple styles along with the larger versions.

Solutions are not always unique. It's not uncommon for four squares on two rows (such as 2, 4 and 4, 2) to be interchangeable. This happens more often in larger puzzles.

Having Fun with More Puzzles

The following puzzles offer a mix of skip puzzles. In each, you solve the puzzle by placing digits and skips. Each row and column has exactly one of each number plus the specified count of skips. Hints around the sides show the nearest number. They pass through skips to get to that number. Use logic and cunning to fill the grid and solve each game.

Puzzle 1

Complete the grid with the digits 1–3, and a single skip (–).

◇		2		1	◇
1		2			—
2			—	1	1
3	3			2	
		—			3
◇			2	3	◇

Puzzle 2

Use the digits 1–3 and a skip (–) to fill this grid.

Puzzle 3

Solve this puzzle using the digits 1–4 and a skip (–).

Puzzle 4

Complete this grid using the digits 1–4 and a skip (–).

◇	4	3	1	3		◇
4	4	3	1	–		2
	2			3		1
	3	2	4			
					3	
		–	3	2		4
◇		1	3	2		◇

Puzzle 5

Solve this skip puzzle using the digits 1–3 and two skips (–).

◇		1	1			◇
	–	–		2		3
		1	–	3		3
	1	–		–	2	2
	3					
	–	3	2	–	1	
◇		3			1	◇

Puzzle 6

This puzzle uses the digits 1–4 and two skips (–).

◇		2		1	4	1	◇
	2	3				1	1
	2			1		4	
			4	3			
	3			1	4	2	
1	1	4				3	–
		1	–	2	–	3	
◇	4	1		2	3	3	◇

Puzzle 7

Solve this puzzle with the digits 1–4 and two skips (–).

◇		3			2		◇
	4	–		1			3
	2		–	4	1	–	1
1	1		3	–	–		
1	–	1		2	3	–	
	–				–		
3		–	2	–	4		
◇	3					1	◇

Puzzle 8

Use the numbers 1–4 and two skips (–) to complete this puzzle.

◇		1	2			1	◇
	3		2		–	–	4
4		–	4	3		1	
1			3	–	4	–	
	2	–				4	4
	4			1		2	
				2	1	3	3
◇	4	4			1	3	◇

Puzzle 9

Complete the grid using the numbers 1–5 and a single skip (–).

◇		1	4	2	3	5	◇
1	–				3	5	5
	3				4		
			1	3	2		4
	4		–	5	1		2
2	2	5		4		1	1
			2			3	3
◇	1	4	2	4	5	3	◇

Puzzle 10

Enter the digits 1–5 and one skip (–) into the grid to complete this puzzle.

◇	2	4	3		4	5	◇
			3	1		5	5
			–		4	1	
	–		4	3		2	
		2			3		3
1		–	5		3		
3		1	2	–		4	4
◇	3		2		5		◇

Puzzle 11

Complete this grid using the digits 1–6 and two skips (–).

◇		4	5	2		3	6	6	◇
1		4		2		3		–	
	3				5	4		–	4
5			–	1	4		3		
2				4	–	5	1		
	–		4		6			2	
		–	3			6	4	1	1
6	6							4	
4						2			
◇	4	1		3	3	6	2		◇

Puzzle 12

Use the numbers 1–6 and two skips (–) to solve this puzzle.

◇	3	1	2	3	6	5	4		◇
		1	2				4	–	
			4	1	5	–	–	6	
2		5	1		–	3	6	4	
	5			6	–	4	1	2	
1	1	–	5		2		–	3	
6	–		3			–	2		
	6	4	–	2	3	1	5	–	
4			6		1	2	3		
◇	4	4		2	1	2		5	◇

Solutions

Here are solutions for each of the puzzles. Don't forget: some solutions are not unique, so your answers might differ from mine.

Puzzle 1

◇	1	2	3	1	◇
1	1	2	3	–	3
2	2	3	–	1	1
3	3	–	1	2	2
1	–	1	2	3	3
◇	3	1	2	3	◇

Puzzle 2

◇	3	1	1	2	◇
3	3	1	–	2	2
2	2	3	1	–	1
2	–	2	3	1	1
1	1	–	2	3	3
◇	1	2	2	3	◇

Puzzle 3

◇	1	3	4	2	3	◇
1	1	–	4	2	3	3
3	–	3	2	1	4	4
4	4	1	3	–	2	2
2	2	4	–	3	1	1
3	3	2	1	4	–	4
◇	3	2	1	4	1	◇

Puzzle 4

◇	4	3	1	3	2	◇
4	4	3	1	–	2	2
2	2	4	–	3	1	1
3	3	2	4	1	–	1
1	–	1	2	4	3	3
1	1	–	3	2	4	4
◇	1	1	3	2	4	◇

Puzzle 5

◇	2	1	1	2	3	◇
1	–	–	1	2	3	3
2	2	1	–	3	–	3
1	1	–	3	–	2	2
3	3	2	–	1	–	1
3	–	3	2	–	1	1
◇	3	3	2	1	1	◇

Puzzle 6

◇	2	2	3	1	4	1	◇
2	–	2	3	–	4	1	1
2	2	3	–	1	–	4	4
4	–	–	4	3	1	2	2
3	3	–	1	4	2	–	2
1	1	4	2	–	3	–	3
4	4	1	–	2	–	3	3
◇	4	1	2	2	3	3	◇

Puzzle 7

◇	4	3	3	1	2	3	◇
4	4	–	–	1	2	3	3
2	2	3	–	4	1	–	1
1	1	4	3	–	–	2	2
1	–	1	4	2	3	–	3
2	–	2	1	3	–	4	4
3	3	–	2	–	4	1	1
◇	3	2	2	3	4	1	◇

Puzzle 8

◇	3	1	2	4	2	1	◇
3	3	1	2	4	–	–	4
4	–	–	4	3	2	1	1
1	1	2	3	–	4	–	4
2	2	–	1	–	3	4	4
4	4	3	–	1	–	2	2
4	–	4	–	2	1	3	3
◇	4	4	1	2	1	3	◇

Puzzle 9

◇	3	1	4	2	3	5	◇
1	–	1	4	2	3	5	5
3	3	2	5	1	4	–	4
5	5	–	1	3	2	4	4
4	4	3	–	5	1	2	2
2	2	5	3	4	–	1	1
1	1	4	2	–	5	3	3
◇	1	4	2	4	5	3	◇

Puzzle 10

◇	2	4	3	1	4	5	◇
2	2	4	3	1	–	5	5
5	5	3	–	2	4	1	1
5	–	5	4	3	1	2	2
4	4	2	1	5	3	–	3
1	1	–	5	4	2	3	3
3	3	1	2	–	5	4	4
◇	3	1	2	4	5	4	◇

Puzzle 11

◇	1	4	5	2	5	3	6	6	◇
1	1	4	5	2	–	3	6	–	6
3	3	2	1	6	5	4	–	–	4
5	5	–	–	1	4	2	3	6	6
2	2	6	–	4	–	5	1	3	3
3	–	3	4	–	6	1	5	2	2
3	–	–	3	5	2	6	4	1	1
6	6	5	2	3	1	–	–	4	4
4	4	1	6	–	3	–	2	5	5
◇	4	1	6	3	3	6	2	5	◇

Puzzle 12

◇	3	1	2	3	6	5	4	6	◇
1	–	1	2	3	6	5	4	–	4
3	3	2	4	1	5	–	–	6	6
2	2	5	1	–	–	3	6	4	4
5	5	3	–	6	–	4	1	2	2
1	1	–	5	4	2	6	–	3	3
6	–	6	3	5	4	–	2	1	1
6	6	4	–	2	3	1	5	–	5
4	4	–	6	–	1	2	3	5	5
◇	4	4	6	2	1	2	3	5	◇

Balanced Groups

Oh no! Our well-organized numbers have accidentally fallen into a sort function. Separate them back out into five groups with equal sums so we can share them fairly with friends: 1, 3, 3, 4, 4, 4, 4, 6, 7, 8, 9, 11, 17, 23, 24, and 27.

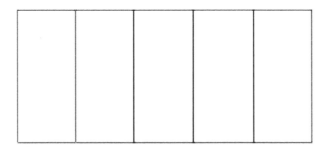

How to Play

Separate the numbers in the puzzle into groups of equal value.

Rules:

- Split the numbers into five groups.
- Balance the values so no bucket is too large or too small.
- The sum for each group is the same across groups.

For more information about this puzzle and its solution, turn the page. When you're ready for more puzzles like this one, see Having Fun with More Puzzles, on page 60.

About This Puzzle

Here's a nice time-waster. You're given a list of sorted numbers. Some are large, others small. Split them apart so they fit into groups of equal value. The sum of each group must balance. You may need to tweak the numbers between sets until they all have the same sum. It's a fun little math puzzle that doesn't take much time to solve and has a bit of crunch for you to enjoy.

Solving the Example

Add all the digits. The sum of these numbers is 155. Divided across five groups leaves a target of 31 per group. You're now set to start work.

Sum: 31

If any numbers are too large to combine, where adding them would result in a sum greater than the target, place them in separate groups.

27	24	23	17	
Sum: 31

The only number that will combine with 27 is 4. 24 is 7 away from 31. You need to add (3, 4) or (6, 1) to the group. Solutions are not unique so either one will do. In a similar way, 23 needs (8), (7, 1) or (4, 4).

27	24	23	17	
4	3 4	4 4		

Sum: 31

After roughing out the solution, it's the fun part. Wiggle around the remaining numbers until your sums are right. It doesn't take long. Once you've solved all but one bucket, the final bucket is already solved for you. Fill it with the remaining numbers.

Sum: 31	27 4	24 3 4	23 4 4	17 1 6 7	3 8 9 11

Background

This puzzle comes straight from my time in grad school. It was a challenge in an algorithms class where you study how to compute answers. Each approach can take more or less time to finish. They also occupy different computer resources. These are important lessons to learn before working as a programmer. Classic problems like these help students understand how to make programs efficient. They're also fun on their own.

I've seen similar puzzles in books, newspapers, and magazines with many stories attached. Some puzzle stories make you split money among a group. You're limited to the bills and coins on hand. Others have valuable minerals or groceries to share. You can't divide the items (no cutting apart coconuts, for example) but the split must be fair to everyone. Underneath the stories, they're group-filling puzzles like the ones in this chapter.

I like these puzzles. They take something unstructured and pack it into neat little bundles. That's so satisfying.

Are you ready to work on some bucket puzzles? Turn the page to get started. I've made a couple a little harder by not telling you how many buckets to use, but they shouldn't be too hard to figure out... Have fun!

Having Fun with More Puzzles

Puzzle 1

Separate these numbers into three groups with equal sums:

3, 11, 21, 26, 36, 44

Puzzle 2

Separate these numbers into three groups with equal sums:

2, 3, 3, 6, 7, 9, 10, 11, 13, 17

Puzzle 3

Separate these numbers into several groups with equal sums:

4, 4, 13, 15, 17, 19, 30

Puzzle 4

Separate these numbers into four groups with equal sums:

1, 2, 3, 5, 5, 9, 11, 12, 15, 15, 15, 17, 17, 21

Puzzle 5

Separate these numbers
into three groups with
equal sums:

3, 4, 7, 8, 9, 11, 14, 14, 19, 28

Puzzle 6

Separate these numbers
into four groups with
equal sums:

2, 3, 7, 9, 12, 15, 15, 16, 17,
21, 26, 28, 29

Puzzle 7

Separate these numbers
into several groups with
equal sums:

4, 6, 6, 11, 11, 14, 16, 17, 20,
23, 27, 29, 31

Puzzle 8

Separate these numbers
into three groups with
equal sums:

13, 16, 18, 18, 22, 25, 49, 61

Solutions

Grouping puzzles may have multiple solutions. Here are answers to every problem, which may or may not exactly match your answers.

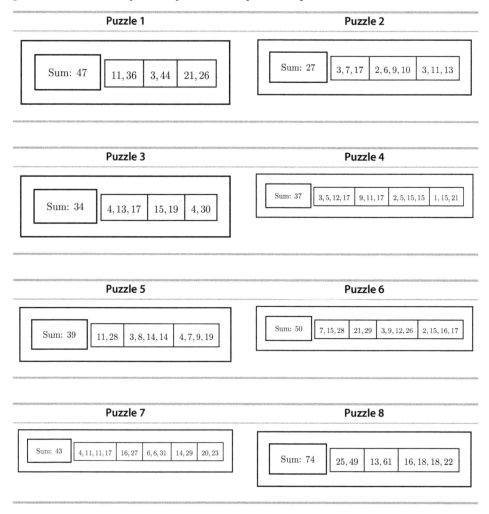

Puzzle 1

Sum: 47 | 11, 36 | 3, 44 | 21, 26

Puzzle 2

Sum: 27 | 3, 7, 17 | 2, 6, 9, 10 | 3, 11, 13

Puzzle 3

Sum: 34 | 4, 13, 17 | 15, 19 | 4, 30

Puzzle 4

Sum: 37 | 3, 5, 12, 17 | 9, 11, 17 | 2, 5, 15, 15 | 1, 15, 21

Puzzle 5

Sum: 39 | 11, 28 | 3, 8, 14, 14 | 4, 7, 9, 19

Puzzle 6

Sum: 50 | 7, 15, 28 | 21, 29 | 3, 9, 12, 26 | 2, 15, 16, 17

Puzzle 7

Sum: 43 | 4, 11, 11, 17 | 16, 27 | 6, 6, 31 | 14, 29 | 20, 23

Puzzle 8

Sum: 74 | 25, 49 | 13, 61 | 16, 18, 18, 22

Magic Triangles

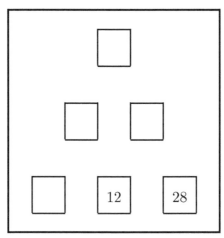

Target: 84

Values: [44, 40, 16, 24]

How to Play

Each side of this triangle has an equal sum. Insert the four values so that each side of the triangle adds up to 84.

For more information about this puzzle and its solution, turn the page. When you're ready for more puzzles like this one, see Having Fun with More Puzzles, on page 68.

About This Puzzle

Magic triangles are numbers laid out in the shape of a triangle's perimeter. The total of every side is equal. That equality makes the triangle "magic." In magic triangle puzzles, some values are left out or deliberately misplaced. You figure out where numbers go so each sum works and the triangle stays magic.

Solving the Example

Let's solve the triangle. The bottom row already has two numbers, so finish that row. Subtracting from 84, the answer must be 44. You can cross out numbers as you use them.

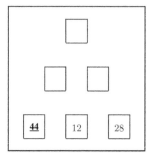

The second row is trickier. There's no simple math left, just logic. Look at the remaining numbers. Two values are pretty close to the ones in the bottom corners: 40 and 44, 24 and 28. Flip them to the opposite side and add them in. Balancing the sides is always a good strategy to try.

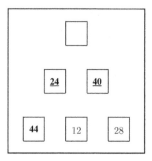

Finish with the final number 16 and check your sums. The total of each side must be equal. If not, go back and make some changes.

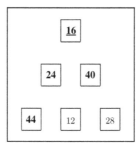

This puzzle is easy. It has only six numbers, and you know all the missing values and the magic sum. Puzzles can use a larger triangle, an unknown total, or missing or misplaced numbers. The small version of magic triangle puzzles is like a one-bite appetizer. More complex puzzles can be a meal.

Interesting Facts

A single magic triangle provides infinite variations. You can add to, subtract from, multiply, or divide by numbers without breaking symmetry. You can rotate and mirror however you like.

Try it yourself. All the original numbers are multiples of 4. Dividing by 4 creates another magic triangle. The new magic number target is 21, which is 84 divided by 4.

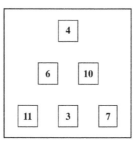

This next triangle subtracts the sample puzzle's numbers from 45. (45 is one more than the largest number in the original.) After subtraction, it's still a magic triangle. The new magic number is 51.

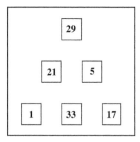

Any math that preserves symmetry in the triangle's values also preserves the "magic" in the triangle. Neat!

Other Shapes

Any polygon, whether a square, a pentagon, a hexagon, and so on, can be magic. Magic polygon possibilities are infinite, with as many sides and numbers per side as you'd like. For example, the following magic octagon contains groups of three numbers on eight sides. Its magic number is 79.

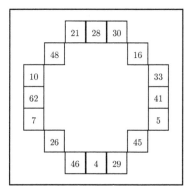

Nor are you limited to three or four values per side. Include as many items as you like (or as your drawing program permits). Check out this next square, for example. Its perimeter includes nine values on each of its four sides. Its magic number is 369. I don't think it would make a very good puzzle with that many numbers but, like the octagon, it is a beautiful thing to look at.

35	25	15	5	76	66	56	46	45
24								34
13								23
2								12
81								1
70								80
59								69
48								58
37	36	26	16	6	77	67	57	47

Having Fun with More Puzzles

Give magic triangle puzzles a try. I put together three styles of puzzles for you:

- Small triangles like the one you've already seen.
- Larger triangles with four numbers per side.
- Mixed-up triangles where two numbers are swapped.

Puzzle 1

Enter the missing values so each triangle side sums to the same value.

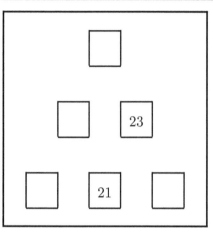

Target: 60

Values: [19, 17, 24, 20]

Puzzle 2

Enter the missing values so each triangle side sums to the same value.

Target: 83

Values: [29, 30, 24, 31]

Puzzle 3

Enter the missing values so each triangle side sums to the same value.

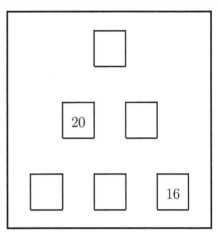

Target: 47

Values: [14, 17, 13, 18]

Puzzle 4

Enter the missing values so each triangle side sums to the same value.

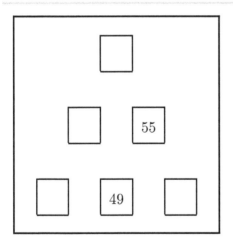

Target: 162

Values: [64, 52, 46, 61]

Puzzle 5

Two values in this magic triangle have swapped positions. Restore them to their original positions so the sum of each side is equal.

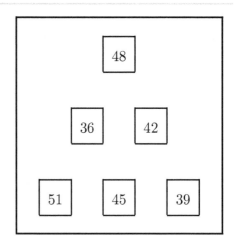

Puzzle 6

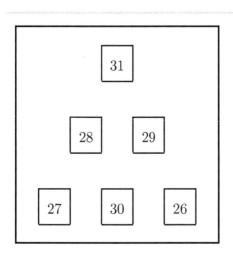

Two values in this magic triangle have swapped positions. Restore them to their original positions so the sum of each side is equal.

Puzzle 7

Two values in this magic triangle have swapped positions. Restore them to their original positions so the sum of each side is equal.

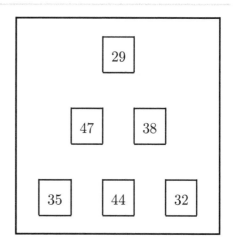

Puzzle 8

Two values in this magic triangle have swapped positions. Restore them to their original positions so the sum of each side is equal.

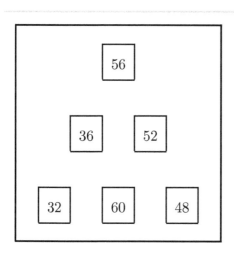

Puzzle 9

Enter the missing values into the puzzle squares so each triangle side sums to the same value.

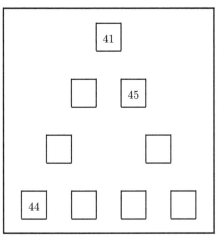

Target: 164

Values: [38, 42, 37, 40, 39, 43]

Puzzle 10

Enter the missing values into the puzzle squares so each triangle side sums to the same value.

Target: 31

Values: [5, 10, 6, 7, 3, 8]

Puzzle 11

Enter the missing values into the puzzle squares so each triangle side sums to the same value.

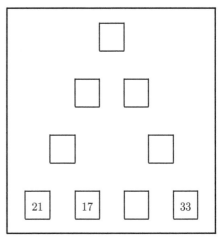

Target: 102

Values: [19, 27, 29, 23, 25, 31]

Puzzle 12

Enter the missing values into the puzzle squares so each triangle side sums to the same value.

Target: 148

Values: [41, 37, 34, 39, 35, 40]

Puzzle 13

Enter the missing values into the puzzle squares so each triangle side sums to the same value.

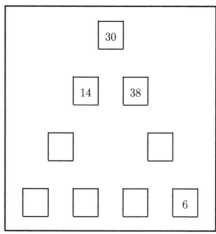

Target: 84

Values: [34, 22, 18, 26, 10]

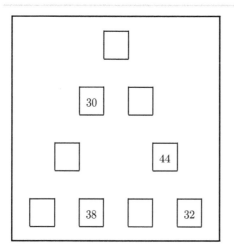

Puzzle 14

Enter the missing values into the puzzle squares so each triangle side sums to the same value.

Target: 146

Values: [36, 42, 34, 28, 40]

Puzzle 15

Enter the missing values into the puzzle squares so each triangle side sums to the same value.

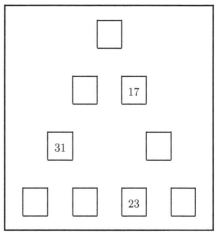

Target: 98

Values: [21, 33, 27, 25, 19, 29]

Puzzle 16

Enter the missing values into the puzzle squares so each triangle side sums to the same value.

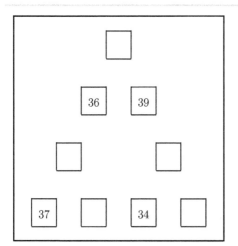

Target: 141

Values: [33, 32, 31, 38, 35]

Solutions

Your answers might differ slightly from these. That's fine. If your magic triangle sums are correct, you've solved the puzzle properly.

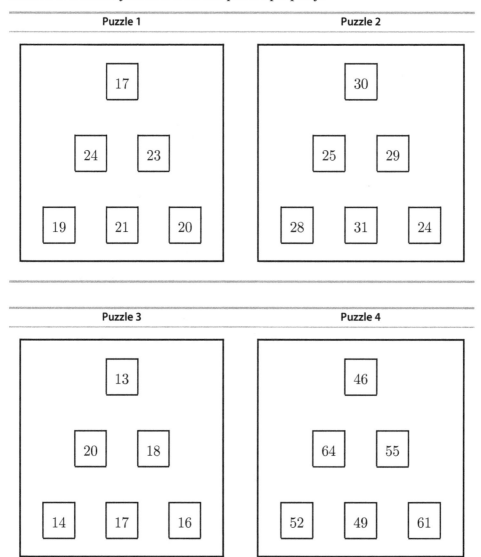

Puzzle 1

17

24 23

19 21 20

Puzzle 2

30

25 29

28 31 24

Puzzle 3

13

20 18

14 17 16

Puzzle 4

46

64 55

52 49 61

Puzzle 5

48

36   42

51   39   45

Puzzle 6

31

28   26

27   30   29

Puzzle 7

29

47   38

35   32   44

Puzzle 8

56

52   36

32   60   48

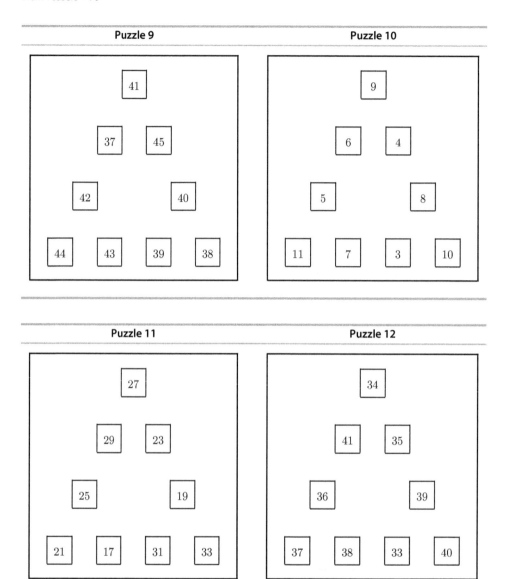

Puzzle 9

41

37 45

42 40

44 43 39 38

Puzzle 10

9

6 4

5 8

11 7 3 10

Puzzle 11

27

29 23

25 19

21 17 31 33

Puzzle 12

34

41 35

36 39

37 38 33 40

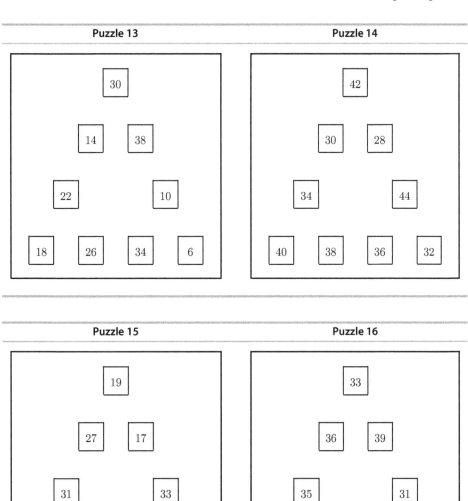

Puzzle 13

30

14   38

22   10

18   26   34   6

Puzzle 14

42

30   28

34   44

40   38   36   32

Puzzle 15

19

27   17

31   33

21   25   23   29

Puzzle 16

33

36   39

35   31

37   32   34   38

Magic Squares

	22	
16		24

How to Play

 In a Magic Square, every row, column, and long diagonal sums to the same number. To solve this puzzle, enter values in each empty space. The magic number for this puzzle, the sum in every direction, is 54.

For more information about this puzzle and its solution, turn the page. When you're ready for more puzzles like this one, see Having Fun with More Puzzles, on page 86.

About This Puzzle

A magic square is a grid of numbers, whose rows, columns, and long diagonals sum to a particular number. For example, this magic square's core sum (called its *magic constant*) is 15.

4	9	2
3	5	7
8	1	6

Add up each row, column, and long diagonal of this grid. Confirm that no matter the direction, the sum remains 15. These sums in their multiple directions add complexity to magic squares. Compare them with the polygons you saw in Puzzle 6, Magic Triangles, on page 63. There, the sums were limited to the numbers along the edges of each shape. Here, the sums fit into two dimensions, not just lines. Keeping these sums consistent, regardless of the size of the square, is both the challenge and the beauty of what makes these squares magical.

A proper magic square has no repeated numbers. Its *order* refers to the size of the square along any side. This example is a magic square of order 3. Magic squares can be of practically any size.

The numbers in this example go from 1 through 9. You can replace these numbers with any consecutive number sequence (like 4, 5, 6, …) or additive number sequence (like 4, 6, 8, …). As long as you keep the same number order, the square remains magic. For example, here's the same square with the numbers 578 to 586. If you have a calculator handy, you can confirm that this square's magic constant is 1746.

581	586	579
580	582	584
585	578	583

The following 4x4 grid contains the numbers 2, 4, 6, 8, and so on up to 32. It is not, however, a magic square. All the rows and columns add up to 68 but its long diagonals do not (48 and 56). To create this almost-magic example,

I "broke" an existing magic square. I moved what is now row two up from the bottom row of a proper magic square. This preserved all the horizontal and vertical sums but I broke the diagonals.

2	30	28	8
26	6	4	32
16	20	22	10
24	12	14	18

If I had mirrored or rotated the magic square, the magic would have remained. It also would by adding a number to every entry or multiplying by a constant. Magic squares are super-cool but they're not indestructible. When I cracked the symmetry, I destroyed the "magic." Magic squares' strong rules make them a fun start for puzzles. As you saw, you have to watch out for near misses. Always check all directions before finishing your solutions.

Solving the Example

In this example, you know the magic constant is 54. Row three already has two numbers. Use subtraction (54 - (16 + 24) = 14) to determine the value. Any row, column, or long diagonal with all but one number can boost you to the next step. Enter 14 into the bottom row's center square. This unlocks the middle column.

	22	
16	**14**	24

Complete the middle column. Add 22 and 14 (36) and subtract from 54 (18). Enter 18 into the middle square.

	22	
	18	
16	**14**	24

Next, work the diagonals. 54 - (24 + 18) is 12. 54 - (16 + 18) is 20. Enter those numbers.

12	22	20
	18	
16	14	24

Finish the two left and right columns. 54 - (12 + 16) is 26. 54 - (20 + 24) is 10.

12	22	20
26	18	10
16	14	24

Check your solution by adding up each row, column, and long diagonal. Every direction must add to 54:

- Top diagonal: 12 + 18 + 24
- Bottom diagonal: 16 + 18 + 20
- Row one: 12 + 22 + 20
- Row two: 26 + 18 + 10
- Row three: 16 + 14 + 24
- Column one: 12 + 26 + 16
- Column two: 22 + 18 + 14
- Column three: 20 + 10 + 24

There are eight different ways to reach 54 using a 3x3 magic square! As the size of each magic square grows larger, the number of sums grows with it. For example, a 4x4 magic square has ten sums, the count of its rows (4), its columns (4), and long diagonals (2).

Background

Magic squares have been around a long time. There's archaeological evidence of their use in China[3] up to four thousand years ago. Magic squares have also been found in ancient India, Europe, and Arabia—squares of antiquity centered on simple sequences, for example, the numbers 1 through 9, or 1

---

3.   https://www.theguardian.com/science/alexs-adventures-in-numberland/2014/nov/04/macaus-magic-square-stamps-just-made-philately-even-more-nerdy

through 16. There's something joyous and, yes, magical about making numbers balance while retaining their identity.

Wikipedia's write-up[4] on magic squares provides many facts on the topic as well as placing them in legends, history, and popular art. *The Joy of Mathematics* by T. Pappas is also an excellent resource for learning more about them.

Magic squares hold a special place in my heart. I used them in some image processing work many years ago for the first paper I ever presented. Returning to magic squares, and using them as a basis for designing puzzles, has been an unexpected pleasure.

Magic squares are like the magic polygons you read about in the previous chapter. Magic squares don't lose their special qualities if you mirror or rotate them. You can multiply and divide each value by the same number or offset their values, and they stay magic. It's another enchanting thing about these marvelous number patterns.

---

4. https://en.wikipedia.org/wiki/Magic_square

Having Fun with More Puzzles

Test yourself with the following magic square puzzles using a couple of puzzle styles. They'll get more challenging as you continue.

Complete these magic squares. Enter each value into one of the empty cells. The horizontal, vertical, and long diagonal sums are the magic constant to the right of each grid.

Puzzle 1

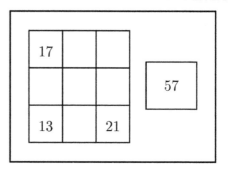

Values: [11, 15, 19, 23, 25, 27]

Puzzle 2

Values: [22, 24, 32, 34, 36, 38]

Puzzle 3

26		30
	24	
	32	

72

Values: [16, 18, 20, 22, 28]

Puzzle 4

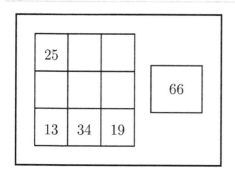

25		
13	34	19

66

Values: [10, 16, 22, 28, 31]

Complete these magic squares. Use the numbers in the grid as clues to solve each puzzle.

Puzzle 5

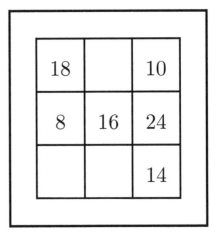

Puzzle 6

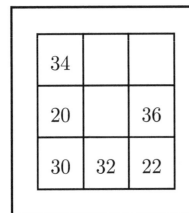

Puzzle 7

25			16
	34		49
		43	
61	19		52

Puzzle 8

31	46	34	67
61	40		
64			
	55	43	58

Our magic squares fell down and two of the numbers accidentally got swapped. Help fix the squares by returning the misplaced numbers to their correct positions!

Puzzle 9

19	39	41	13
29	25	23	35
17	33	31	27
43	15	21	37

Puzzle 10

33	12	27
18	30	24
21	36	15

Puzzle 11

20	35	32
17	29	41
26	23	38

Puzzle 12

33	37	29	39
43	25	15	19
41	27	35	17
21	31	23	45

Complete these magic squares. Enter each value from the list into an empty cell.

Puzzle 13

21	54		57
63	36		
	39		
30		33	66

Values: [24, 27, 42, 45, 48, 51, 60]

Puzzle 14

16	28	26	
24			30
	34		8

Values: [10, 12, 14, 18, 20, 22, 32, 36, 38]

Puzzle 15

			14
30		24	36
		32	
	16		38

Values: [18, 20, 22, 26, 28, 34, 40, 42, 44]

Puzzle 16

30	28			
	32		18	56
12	50	48	36	
	14	52	40	

Values: [10, 16, 20, 22, 24, 26, 34, 38, 42, 44, 46, 54, 58]

Solutions

While your answers probably match mine, things like symmetry may allow slight changes that are also correct.

Puzzle 1

17	15	25
27	19	11
13	23	21

Puzzle 2

36	22	32
26	30	34
28	38	24

Puzzle 3

26	16	30
28	24	20
18	32	22

Puzzle 4

25	10	31
28	22	16
13	34	19

Puzzle 5

18	20	10
8	16	24
22	12	14

Puzzle 6

34	24	26
20	28	36
30	32	22

Puzzle 7

25	55	58	16
40	34	31	49
28	46	43	37
61	19	22	52

Puzzle 8

31	46	34	67
61	40	52	25
64	37	49	28
22	55	43	58

Puzzle 9

19	39	41	13
29	25	23	35
21	33	31	27
43	15	17	37

Puzzle 10

33	12	27
18	24	30
21	36	15

Puzzle 11

20	35	32
41	29	17
26	23	38

Puzzle 12

15	37	29	39
43	25	33	19
41	27	35	17
21	31	23	45

Puzzle 13

21	54	42	57
63	36	48	27
60	39	51	24
30	45	33	66

Puzzle 14

38	10	12	32
16	28	26	22
24	20	18	30
14	34	36	8

Puzzle 15

20	40	42	14
30	26	24	36
22	34	32	28
44	16	18	38

Puzzle 16

30	28	16	54	42
44	32	20	18	56
58	46	34	22	10
12	50	48	36	24
26	14	52	40	38

Group Grids

6	6			
5			4	
	6		4	3
5			1	6
	6			6

How to Play

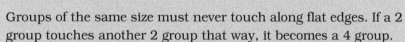

Write a number into each space. Each number is that cell's group size. For example, the number 3 means that three cells connect together along flat edges to form a group. Diagonals don't count when building groups.

Groups of the same size must never touch along flat edges. If a 2 group touches another 2 group that way, it becomes a 4 group.

As you fill out the puzzle, it may help to outline each group with lines. This helps you see each group better.

For more information about this puzzle and its solution, turn the page. When you're ready for more puzzles like this one, see Having Fun with More Puzzles, on page 101.

About This puzzle

Get out your pencil. It's time to play a gameboard-style brain teaser. Group grids are puzzles made up of numbers and empty spaces in a 2D matrix. You write numbers in each empty space. Hints are all over the puzzle board to help you. To reiterate the rules:

- Each number shows a cell's group size. The number 3 means that three cells connect together to form a group.

- Groups connect across sides but not diagonals.

- Groups of the same size never touch.

Solving the Example

When working on these puzzles, look for small groups with few choices. For example, check out the 3 on the right. The only way to move is up. After that, you can't move on diagonals so the single choice for the 3-group is straight up, making a little line.

6	6			**3**
5			4	**3**
	6		4	3
5			1	6
	6			6

Now consider the 6s. They're all over the board, so probably not one group. More likely, the way the 6s sit means there will be two distinct groups that can't touch. The 6 halfway down the second column may belong to the top or bottom group. It also looks like one group of 4 and one of 5.

Most puzzles have more than one solution. If you push the 4s to the left, the top-left 6s have to fill out the first row. If you push the 4s up, the 6s squeeze into the spaces next to the 4s. Choose as you like.

6	6	6	6	3
5	6	4	4	3
	6	4	4	3
5			1	6
	6			6

The 5s can only fill up the rest of the first two columns. That leaves everything else as 6. Puzzle done.

6	6	6	6	3
5	6	4	4	3
5	6	4	4	3
5	5	6	1	6
5	6	6	6	6

Now that the board is full, look at the groups of 4 and 6 on the top half. Notice this: you can't flip the 6 at the top right with the 4 in the center. If you did, the two groups of 6s would connect. That makes a group of 12, not two groups of 6. Take care that groups with the same count don't touch. (You can, however, flip that 6 with the 4 on the *second* row.)

This was a small puzzle, just 5x5. As they grow in size, group puzzles become more complex with more choices, and you may need to backtrack. Small puzzles are quicker than large ones, while bigger puzzles provide more challenge.

I love the satisfaction of thinking through these puzzles. I fill the spaces where I know certain numbers *must* be, and then I focus on what-ifs. I find it helps to work from the edges, moving inward. That way you don't end up with orphan spaces you can't fill.

Background

These puzzles began with my work in building game maps. It's surprisingly hard to fill spaces with interesting shapes. You need more than squares in there and you don't want the first few shapes to take up all the room.

I found I created much nicer maps with small groups different from their neighbors. The same applied as I made the maps smaller and smaller. That's where the "no-touching" rule for these puzzles comes from.

For those of you interested in these things, here's a little background. To make each puzzle, I pick a random point and squeeze each new group into my grid, like a frosting bag. As I inject, I pick random edges to grow. I also roll a D20 die for a number between 1 and 20. D20 dice[5] are used in roleplaying games. They provide more variety in rolled numbers than six-sided dice. If the number rolled is greater than 15, I stop. This lets me build those groups of different sizes, one after the other. That's key for this puzzle. Too many groups of the same size don't make good puzzles, or good maps.

I also check to make sure that each new group fits my rules. Does it touch another group of the same size? For maps, where it matters, is it compact enough? If the group fails my tests, I erase it and try again.

These puzzles have a certain popularity. I've seen space-filling grid puzzles online and in magazines. Popular versions of similar games appear under the names Fillomino and Allied Occupation. The rules vary. Some focus on the boundaries separating each group. Some tell you the area of the group but limit you to working with rectangles. Others won't let groups touch, regardless of size. Instead, you must leave spaces between them on the map.

I prefer the style I share with you in this chapter. They're quick to solve but they still create a challenge. I prefer to design puzzles that are simpler than, say, crosswords or 9x9-square Sudoku. They demand less of your time but still provide that click of mental satisfaction.

I think what makes group grid puzzles nice is balance. A good one has enough rules to let you solve them but few enough clues to keep them interesting.

---

5. https://en.wikipedia.org/wiki/D20_System

Having Fun with More Puzzles

Now that you've seen how group grids work, try them out for yourself. They vary from small and simple to larger and more challenging.

An answer key follows the puzzles.

Puzzle 1

3		6	6	1
			6	
	4	5		
6	4	6		5
			6	

Puzzle 2

2		4		
	5	4		
	5		5	5
	3			6
		6	6	

Puzzle 3

	6	6	1	6	1	
6		1	6		6	
	1	5	4	4		
4				5	6	
4				6		6

Puzzle 4

6			3			
	6	5			6	1
3	6	5		6	6	
			3		4	4
4		4				

Puzzle 5

4	4		2			4	4
		6		6			
	7	1	8	6			
7		8	8		5	8	8
		8			5		8
	7		3			8	

Puzzle 6

1		7	7			7	1
4	4		5				
			8	1	5	5	
6		5				4	
1		8	8	8	5		
	6	6		5			4

Puzzle 7

1	5		5		6	
	6			2	4	6
	6			4	1	6
6		3		6	6	4
	4		4		6	
	5		5		1	4

Puzzle 8

		5	5		7	7
3				7		2
7	7			1		
7		4		6	6	6
		4			1	
5			5	7	7	7

Solutions

Here are answers to the puzzles for this chapter. Group puzzles may sometimes have more than one solution.

Puzzle 1

3	6	6	6	1
3	4	4	6	6
3	4	5	5	6
6	4	6	5	5
6	6	6	6	5

Puzzle 2

2	2	4	4	5
5	5	4	5	5
5	5	4	5	5
5	3	6	6	6
3	3	6	6	6

Puzzle 3

6	6	6	1	6	1	6
6	6	1	6	6	6	6
6	1	5	4	4	4	4
4	5	5	5	5	6	6
4	4	4	6	6	6	6

Puzzle 4

6	6	6	3	3	6	6
6	6	5	5	3	6	1
3	6	5	5	6	6	6
3	3	5	3	3	4	4
4	4	4	4	3	4	4

Puzzle 5

4	4	4	2	2	6	4	4
4	7	6	6	6	6	8	4
7	7	1	8	6	5	8	4
7	8	8	8	5	5	8	8
7	8	8	8	5	5	8	8
7	7	8	3	3	3	8	8

Puzzle 6

1	4	7	7	7	7	7	1
4	4	5	5	7	5	7	5
4	5	5	8	1	5	5	5
6	6	5	8	8	8	4	4
1	6	8	8	8	5	5	4
6	6	6	8	5	5	5	4

Puzzle 7

1	5	5	5	2	6	6	6
6	6	5	5	2	4	6	6
6	6	6	4	4	4	1	6
6	3	3	3	6	6	6	4
4	4	4	4	6	6	4	4
5	5	5	5	5	6	1	4

Puzzle 8

3	3	5	5	5	7	7	7
3	7	5	5	7	7	7	2
7	7	7	4	1	7	6	2
7	7	4	4	6	6	6	6
7	5	4	7	7	1	6	7
5	5	5	5	7	7	7	7

Water Pails

You're given a 5-pint bucket, an 8-pint bucket, and an unlimited source of water. Starting with empty buckets, measure exactly 2 pints of water.

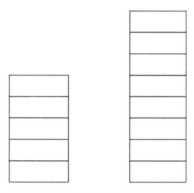

How to Play

Using the buckets and the water supply, measure out your water. Choose from these three actions for each step:

- Fill up either pail with water to the top.
- Empty an entire pail onto the ground.
- Pour one pail into the other pail until the receiving pail is full. There may be water left in the pouring pail after the other pail is full.

For more information about this puzzle and its solution, turn the page. When you're ready for more puzzles like this one, see Having Fun with More Puzzles, on page 114.

About This Puzzle

Water pail puzzles are a classic math problem. You're given two containers and an unlimited supply of water. You work out how to produce an exact quantity of water. It's fun but never as easy as just filling up one pail or the other.

Use math and deduction skills to work your way to a solution. The keys are planning, subtraction, and empty spaces. These puzzles are tricky but engaging. As the container volumes grow, you'll need to use and reuse space and water in ever more clever ways.

Can you work through all the quantities you need only by pouring and filling water? Yes, and the answers aren't complex. Figuring out those steps is where all the fun lies.

For example, say one pail holds 5 gallons and the other pail holds 7. You can fill the larger pail and use it to fill the smaller one. This leaves exactly 2 gallons in the larger 7-gallon pail. This kind of sequence helps you work toward your goal.

Solving the Example

Here's how to measure 2 pints using a 5-pint bucket and an 8-pint bucket. There are many solutions for each puzzle. The best answers use the fewest possible steps. Aim for those short solutions with less work.

Start with the empty 5-pint bucket
and an empty 8-pint bucket.

Fill the 5-pint bucket.

Pour the entire 5-pint bucket into the
8-pint bucket.

Fill the 5-pint bucket, again.

Fill the 8-pint bucket from the 5-pint bucket, which currently has 5 pints in it. Only 3 more pints will fit in the 8-pint bucket.

These steps leave 2 pints in the 5-pint bucket. Set aside the 8-pint bucket. The 2 pints in the 5-pint bucket solves the puzzle.

As you can see from this example, use and think about negative space. After the first pour, there's 3 pints of space in the 8-pint bucket. This space allows you to split the contents of a full 5-pint bucket into 3 and 2.

In these puzzles, you don't need any tools other than your buckets. You never have to measure the pour beyond filling and emptying. Knowing "eight minus five is three" and "five minus three is two" gives you all the math you need.

Water Pails, State, and Math

All filling puzzles revolve around the sizes of the two containers. That's because there are many unsolvable puzzle scenarios. For example, if you have a 6-liter bottle and an 4-liter bottle, can you measure out exactly 1 liter? The answer is no, but why?

Water pail puzzles rely on the greatest common denominator (GCD) of the containers. The GCD is the largest integer that can divide any pair of two numbers. This determines the smallest unit you can separate out. For 6 and 4, the GCD is 2. With a 6-liter bottle and a 4-liter bottle, you can measure 2, 4, 6, 8, and 10 liters but not 1. You'll find puzzles with 7- and 9-unit containers (where the GCD is 1) but rarely ones with 6- and 8-unit ones (GCD 2) or 6- and 9-unit ones (GCD 3) because the target must always be a multiple of the GCD.

Here's another thing to think about. Water filling puzzle solutions are never unique. At any point in the solve, you can swap some water back and forth, over and over. This means there are always an infinite number of possible solutions. Some of them are just silly. For the best solutions, try not to backtrack.

All solutions have a simple math basis. With two containers and the three rules, there's a fixed number of *states*. A state shows the values of a puzzle as you solve it. For water filling puzzles, the amount in each bucket at any point is its state.

For example, if the 6-liter bottle contains 4 liters and the 4-liter bottle is empty, the state is (4, 0). The order tells you which bottle is which and the numbers say how many units are in each bottle. (I put the 6-liter state first to simplify drawing upcoming diagrams. The order doesn't matter. Just be consistent.)

Working from a start state (the puzzle) to an end state (the solution) describes the pouring and filling steps. If you want to, you can compute all possible moves and all distributions of water: every possible pathway and every possible state that exists.

I'll walk through an example of this in the next section, which is a little spoiler-y.

State Graphs

One way to show puzzle states is by drawing a graph. For two-container water puzzles, a grid works well. Mine is slanted to look pretty but normal graph paper also works. The number pairs around the edges represent states. This is the state diagram for the 6-liter, 4-liter puzzle.

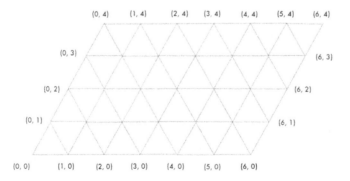

Every state's label shows two numbers in parentheses. The first number is the contents of the 6-liter bottle, the second the 4-liter bottle. The start point is the (0,0) state at the bottom left. This stands for two empty bottles.

There are two rules for moving through this graph:

- Move completely across the graph. You can't stop part way. This corresponds to emptying or filling a bottle.

- Don't backtrack. Once you've filled out a line, don't repeat it. The solution is already on the graph. You can take a different path from any point you've reached. This is a different choice: filling or emptying a bucket, or pouring one bucket into another.

Let me work through this with you to show why certain states aren't reachable. If you fill the 4-liter bottle, you end up at the top-left, the 6-liter at the bottom-right. From there, you can:

- Fill the 6-liter bottle from the 4 (0, 4) -> (4, 0)

- Fill the 4-liter bottle from the 6-liter bottle, leaving 2 liters in the 6-liter bottle (6, 0) -> (2, 4)

- Fill the other bottle, so both are full (6, 0) -> (6, 4), or (0, 4) -> (6, 4)

If, instead, you empty either bottle, you return to the bottom left (0, 0). This breaks rule two. I've highlighted the lines for each action and circled the visited states.

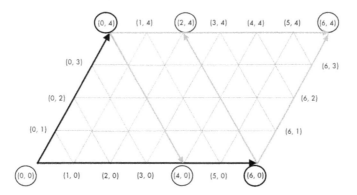

Following the two rules allows you move from state to state to state. You will soon complete the graph. Now you can better see the issue using two containers with even volumes:

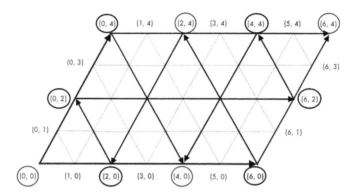

This graph is finished. It never visited any state with an odd number. Those states are unreachable using this pair of bottles. To contrast, consider Puzzle 6 from this chapter. (This is the spoiler bit.)

Puzzle 6 reads, "You have a 4-pint container and a 7-pint container and unlimited water. Measure out 9 pints of water." With a GCD of 1, it's solvable for every value from 1 to 11. The 7-pint number appears first in each state. That makes the graph wider than higher, and drawing the graph easier for this book—tall images take up too much vertical space.

For 9 pints total, there are two possible solution states: (5, 4) and (7, 2). The answer key uses the (5, 4) state and so does this graph. It mirrors the steps exactly from that solution.

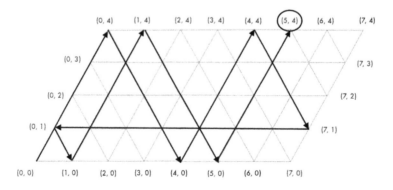

The solution is:

- Start with an empty 4-pint container and an empty 7-pint container. (0, 0)

- Fill the 4-pint container. (0, 4)

- Pour the entire 4-pint container into the 7-pint container. (4, 0)

- Fill the 4-pint container. (4, 4)

- Pour 3 pints from the 4-pint container to fill the 7-pint container. This leaves 1 pint in the 4-pint container. (7, 1)

- Empty the 7-pint container. (0, 1)

- There is 1 pint in the 4-pint container. Empty the 4-pint container into the 7-pint container. (1, 0)

- Fill the 4-pint container. (1, 4)

- Pour the entire 4-pint container into the 7-pint container. The 7-pint container now contains 5 pints. (5, 0)

- Fill the 4-pint container. (5, 4)

If you want to reach (7, 2) instead, fill the 7-pint container from the 4-pint container. This leaves 2 pints in the 4-pint container. Unlike the (6, 4) graph, keep tracing and you *will* eventually reach every state.

Having Fun with More Puzzles

Here are some puzzles that invite you to reason through measurements. They start simply and then ramp up the challenge.

Puzzle 1

Given a 5-liter container and an 8-liter container and an unlimited source of water, measure exactly 10 liters of water.

Puzzle 2

You're given a 4-gallon jar and a 9-gallon jar and unlimited water. Measure out 1 gallon of water.

Puzzle 3

You have a 4-liter container and a 9-liter container and an unlimited water source. Measure exactly 10 liters of water.

Puzzle 4

Given a 5-pint jar and a 7-pint jar and an unlimited source of water, measure exactly 4 pints of water.

Puzzle 5

You're given a 4-ounce bucket and a 5-ounce bucket and an unlimited source of water. Measure exactly 2 ounces of water.

Puzzle 6

You have a 4-pint container and a 7-pint container and unlimited water. Measure out 9 pints of water.

Puzzle 7

You're given a 3-gallon pail and an 8-gallon pail and an unlimited source of water. Measure exactly 1 gallon of water.

Puzzle 8

Given a 3-pint jar and a 7-pint jar and unlimited water, measure exactly 8 pints of water.

Puzzle 9

You're given a 5-ounce bucket and a 9-ounce bucket and an unlimited source of water. Measure exactly 8 ounces of water.

Puzzle 10

You have one 3-ounce glass and one 10-ounce glass plus unlimited water. Measure out 11 ounces of water.

Puzzle 11

With a 5-ounce jar and an 8-ounce jar and an unlimited source of water, measure exactly 6 ounces of water.

Puzzle 12

You're given a 7-ounce pail and an 11-ounce pail and an unlimited source of water. Measure exactly 1 ounce of water.

Puzzle 13

Use an 8-ounce pail and a 15-ounce pail and unlimited water to measure out 2 ounces of water.

Puzzle 14

Given a 7-pint glass and a 15-pint glass and unlimited water, measure out exactly 18 pints of water.

Puzzle 15

You're given a 7-pint glass and a 15-pint glass and an unlimited source of water. Measure exactly 12 pints of water.

Solutions

These solutions solve each container problem. They may not exactly match your answers. They should get you to the answer in a simple way.

Puzzle 1

A solution for measuring 10 liters from a 5-liter container and an 8-liter container:

- Start with an empty 5-liter container and an empty 8-liter container.
- Fill the 5-liter container.
- Pour the entire 5-liter container into the 8-liter container.
- Fill the 5-liter container.

There are 10 liters in the two containers: 5 in the 5-liter container and 5 in the 8-liter container.

Puzzle 2

A solution for measuring 1 gallon from a 4-gallon jar and a 9-gallon jar:

- Start with an empty 4-gallon jar and an empty 9-gallon jar.
- Fill the 9-gallon jar.
- Fill the 4-gallon jar by pouring 4 gallons from the 9-gallon jar, leaving 5 gallons in the 9-gallon jar.
- Empty the 4-gallon jar.
- Fill the 4-gallon jar by pouring 4 gallons from the 9-gallon jar, leaving 1 gallon in the 9-gallon jar.

Set aside the 4-gallon jar. There is 1 gallon in the 9-gallon jar.

Puzzle 3

A solution for measuring 10 liters from a 4-liter container and a 9-liter container:

- Start with an empty 4-liter container and an empty 9-liter container.

- Fill the 9-liter container.

- Pour 4 liters from the 9-liter container to fill the 4-liter container. This leaves 5 liters in the 9-liter container.

- Empty the 4-liter container.

- Fill the 4-liter container by pouring 4 liters from the 9-liter container. This leaves 1 liter in the 9-liter container.

- Empty the 4-liter container.

- There is 1 liter in the 9-liter container. Empty the 9-liter container into the 4-liter container.

- Fill the 9-liter container.

There are 10 liters in the two containers: 1 in the 4-liter container and 9 in the 9-liter container.

Puzzle 4

A solution for measuring 4 pints from a 5-pint jar and a 7-pint jar:

- Start with an empty 5-pint jar and an empty 7-pint jar.

- Fill the 7-pint jar.

- Fill the 5-pint jar by pouring 5 pints from the 7-pint jar, leaving 2 pints in the 7-pint jar.

- Empty the 5-pint jar.

- There are 2 pints in the 7-pint jar. Empty the 7-pint jar into the 5-pint jar.

- Fill the 7-pint jar.

- Fill the 5-pint jar by pouring 3 pints from the 7-pint jar, leaving 4 pints in the 7-pint jar.

Puzzle 5

A solution for measuring 2 ounces from a 4-ounce bucket and a 5-ounce bucket:

- Start with an empty 4-ounce bucket and an empty 5-ounce bucket.

- Fill the 5-ounce bucket.

- Fill the 4-ounce bucket by pouring 4 ounces from the 5-ounce bucket, leaving 1 ounce in the 5-ounce bucket.

- Empty the 4-ounce bucket.

- There is 1 ounce in the 5-ounce bucket. Empty the 5-ounce bucket into the 4-ounce bucket.

- Fill the 5-ounce bucket.

- Fill the 4-ounce bucket by pouring 3 ounces from the 5-ounce bucket, leaving 2 ounces in the 5-ounce bucket.

Set aside the 4-ounce bucket. There are 2 ounces in the 5-ounce bucket.

Puzzle 6

A solution for measuring 9 pints from a 4-pint container and a 7-pint container:

- Start with an empty 4-pint container and an empty 7-pint container.

- Fill the 4-pint container.

- Pour the entire 4-pint container into the 7-pint container.

- Fill the 4-pint container.

- Fill the 7-pint container with 3 pints from the 4-pint container, leaving 1 pint in the 4-pint container.

- Empty the 7-pint container.

- There is 1 pint in the 4-pint container. Empty the 4-pint container into the 7-pint container.

- Fill the 4-pint container.

- Pour the entire 4-pint container into the 7-pint container. The 7-pint container now contains 5 pints.

- Fill the 4-pint container.

There are 9 pints in the two containers: 4 in the 4-pint container and 5 in the 7-pint container.

Puzzle 7

A solution for measuring 1 gallon from a 3-gallon pail and an 8-gallon pail:

- Start with an empty 3-gallon pail and an empty 8-gallon pail.

- Fill the 3-gallon pail.

- Pour the entire 3-gallon pail into the 8-gallon pail.

- Fill the 3-gallon pail.

- Pour the entire 3-gallon pail into the 8-gallon pail. The 8-gallon pail now contains 6 gallons.

- Fill the 3-gallon pail.

- Fill the 8-gallon pail by pouring 2 gallons from the 3-gallon pail, leaving 1 gallon in the 3-gallon pail.

Set aside the 8-gallon pail. There is 1 gallon in the 3-gallon pail.

Puzzle 8

A solution for measuring 8 pints from a 3-pint jar and a 7-pint jar:

- Start with an empty 3-pint jar and an empty 7-pint jar.

- Fill the 7-pint jar.

- Fill the 3-pint jar by pouring 3 pints from the 7-pint jar, leaving 4 pints in the 7-pint jar.

- Empty the 3-pint jar.

- Fill the 3-pint jar by pouring 3 pints from the 7-pint jar, leaving 1 pint in the 7-pint jar.

- Empty the 3-pint jar.

- There is 1 pint in the 7-pint jar. Empty the 7-pint jar into the 3-pint jar.

- Fill the 7-pint jar.

There are 8 pints in the two jars: 1 in the 3-pint jar and 7 in the 7-pint jar.

Puzzle 9

A solution for measuring 8 ounces from a 5-ounce bucket and a 9-ounce bucket:

- Start with an empty 5-ounce bucket and an empty 9-ounce bucket.

- Fill the 9-ounce bucket.

- Fill the 5-ounce bucket by pouring 5 ounces from the 9-ounce bucket, leaving 4 ounces in the 9-ounce bucket.

- Empty the 5-ounce bucket.

- There are 4 ounces in the 9-ounce bucket. Empty the 9-ounce bucket into the 5-ounce bucket.

- Fill the 9-ounce bucket.

- Fill the 5-ounce bucket by pouring 1 ounce from the 9-ounce bucket, leaving 8 ounces in the 9-ounce bucket.

Set aside the 5-ounce bucket. There are 8 ounces in the 9-ounce bucket.

Puzzle 10

A solution for measuring 11 ounces from a 3-ounce glass and a 10-ounce glass:

- Start with an empty 3-ounce glass and an empty 10-ounce glass.

- Fill the 10-ounce glass.

- Fill the 3-ounce glass by pouring 3 ounces from the 10-ounce glass, leaving 7 ounces in the 10-ounce glass.

- Empty the 3-ounce glass.

- Fill the 3-ounce glass by pouring 3 ounces from the 10-ounce glass, leaving 4 ounces in the 10-ounce glass.

- Empty the 3-ounce glass.

- Fill the 3-ounce glass by pouring 3 ounces from the 10-ounce glass, leaving 1 ounce in the 10-ounce glass.

- Empty the 3-ounce glass.

- There is 1 ounce in the 10-ounce glass. Empty the 10-ounce glass into the 3-ounce glass.

- Fill the 10-ounce glass.

There are 11 ounces in the two glasses: 1 in the 3-ounce glass and 10 in the 10-ounce glass.

Puzzle 11

A solution for measuring 6 ounces from a 5-ounce jar and an 8-ounce jar:

- Start with an empty 5-ounce jar and an empty 8-ounce jar.

- Fill the 8-ounce jar.

- Fill the 5-ounce jar by pouring 5 ounces from the 8-ounce jar, leaving 3 ounces in the 8-ounce jar.

- Empty the 5-ounce jar.

- There are 3 ounces in the 8-ounce jar. Empty the 8-ounce jar into the 5-ounce jar.

- Fill the 8-ounce jar.

- Fill the 5-ounce jar by pouring 2 ounces from the 8-ounce jar, leaving 6 ounces in the 8-ounce jar.

Set aside the 5-ounce jar. There are 6 ounces in the 8-ounce jar.

Puzzle 12

A solution for measuring 1 ounce from a 7-ounce pail and an 11-ounce pail:

- Start with an empty 7-ounce pail and an empty 11-ounce pail.

- Fill the 11-ounce pail.

- Fill the 7-ounce pail by pouring 7 ounces from the 11-ounce pail, leaving 4 ounces in the 11-ounce pail.

- Empty the 7-ounce pail.

- There are 4 ounces in the 11-ounce pail. Empty the 11-ounce pail into the 7-ounce pail.

- Fill the 11-ounce pail.

- Fill the 7-ounce pail by pouring 3 ounces from the 11-ounce pail, leaving 8 ounces in the 11-ounce pail.

- Empty the 7-ounce pail.

- Fill the 7-ounce pail by pouring 7 ounces from the 11-ounce pail, leaving 1 ounce in the 11-ounce pail.

Set aside the 7-ounce pail. There is 1 ounce in the 11-ounce pail.

Puzzle 13

A solution for measuring 2 ounces from an 8-ounce pail and a 15-ounce pail:

- Start with an empty 8-ounce pail and an empty 15-ounce pail.

- Fill the 8-ounce pail.

- Pour the entire 8-ounce pail into the 15-ounce pail.

- Fill the 8-ounce pail.

- Fill the 15-ounce pail by pouring 7 ounces from the 8-ounce pail, leaving 1 ounce in the 8-ounce pail.

- Empty the 15-ounce pail.

- There is 1 ounce in the 8-ounce pail. Empty the 8-ounce pail into the 15-ounce pail.

- Fill the 8-ounce pail.

- Pour the entire 8-ounce pail into the 15-ounce pail. The 15-ounce pail now contains 9 ounces.

- Fill the 8-ounce pail.

- Fill the 15-ounce pail by pouring 6 ounces from the 8-ounce pail, leaving 2 ounces in the 8-ounce pail.

Set aside the 15-ounce pail. There are 2 ounces in the 8-ounce pail.

Puzzle 14

A solution for measuring 18 pints from a 7-pint glass and a 15-pint glass:

- Start with an empty 7-pint glass and an empty 15-pint glass.

- Fill the 15-pint glass.

- Fill the 7-pint glass by pouring 7 pints from the 15-pint glass, leaving 8 pints in the 15-pint glass.

- Empty the 7-pint glass.

- Fill the 7-pint glass by pouring 7 pints from the 15-pint glass, leaving 1 pint in the 15-pint glass.

- Empty the 7-pint glass.

- There is 1 pint in the 15-pint glass. Empty the 15-pint glass into the 7-pint glass.

- Fill the 15-pint glass.

- Fill the 7-pint glass by pouring 6 pints from the 15-pint glass, leaving 9 pints in the 15-pint glass.

- Empty the 7-pint glass.

- Fill the 7-pint glass by pouring 7 pints from the 15-pint glass, leaving 2 pints in the 15-pint glass.

- Empty the 7-pint glass.

- There are 2 pints in the 15-pint glass. Empty the 15-pint glass into the 7-pint glass.

- Fill the 15-pint glass.

- Fill the 7-pint glass by pouring 5 pints from the 15-pint glass, leaving 10 pints in the 15-pint glass.

- Empty the 7-pint glass.

- Fill the 7-pint glass by pouring 7 pints from the 15-pint glass, leaving 3 pints in the 15-pint glass.

- Empty the 7-pint glass.

- There are 3 pints in the 15-pint glass. Empty the 15-pint glass into the 7-pint glass.

- Fill the 15-pint glass.

There are 18 pints in the two glasses: 3 in the 7-pint glass and 15 in the 15-pint glass.

Puzzle 15

A solution for measuring 12 pints from a 7-pint glass and a 15-pint glass:

- Start with an empty 7-pint glass and an empty 15-pint glass.

- Fill the 7-pint glass.

- Pour the entire 7-pint glass into the 15-pint glass.

- Fill the 7-pint glass.

- Pour the entire 7-pint glass into the 15-pint glass. The 15-pint glass now contains 14 pints.

- Fill the 7-pint glass.

- Fill the 15-pint glass by pouring 1 pint from the 7-pint glass, leaving 6 pints in the 7-pint glass.

- Empty the 15-pint glass.

- There are 6 pints in the 7-pint glass. Empty the 7-pint glass into the 15-pint glass.

- Fill the 7-pint glass.

- Pour the entire 7-pint glass into the 15-pint glass. The 15-pint glass now contains 13 pints.

- Fill the 7-pint glass.

- Fill the 15-pint glass by pouring 2 pints from the 7-pint glass, leaving 5 pints in the 7-pint glass.

- Empty the 15-pint glass.

- There are 5 pints in the 7-pint glass. Empty the 7-pint glass into the 15-pint glass.

- Fill the 7-pint glass.

There are 12 pints in the two glasses: 7 in the 7-pint glass and 5 in the 15-pint glass.

Digit Sum Squares

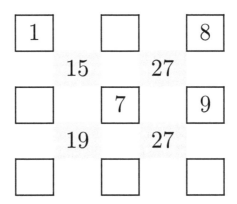

How to Play

 Enter the digits 1 through 9 into the empty squares. Between each group of four digits is a sum. The four digits surrounding those numbers must add up exactly to that value.

For more information about this puzzle and its solution, turn the page. When you're ready for more puzzles like this one, see Having Fun with More Puzzles, on page 133.

About This Puzzle

Digit sum squares offer a quick and engaging challenge. You enter the digits 1 through 9 into empty squares on a 3x3 board. A puzzle shows the sums for each corner of the board. Place the digits to match those sums. It's a fun bit of math and deduction.

Use each digit once, including any pre-filled clues at the start of the puzzle. Given four clues, as in the following sample, you're left with five digits to work with. Each sum adds the four digits that surround it. A completed puzzle means every square is filled with four correct sums.

Solving the Example

Puzzles becomes more challenging with fewer clues. This puzzle has four, which leaves five empty spaces for you to fill. Apart from the pre-filled digits, you must place [2, 3, 4, 5, 6] into the remaining squares.

The number 27 at the top right is already surrounded by three digits. Perform the math, subtracting 8 + 9 + 7 (that is, 24) from 27. This produces the digit 3 to enter into the top-center square.

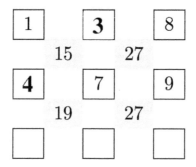

Filling in the 3 then feeds into the top-left set of numbers, 1, 3 and 7. More math: 15 - (1 + 3 + 7) is 4. Enter 4 into the left-middle box. That's two numbers down, and three to go. Your remaining numbers are [2, 5, 6].

The sum clue on the bottom right is 27. You need 11 more, as 27 - (7 + 9) is 11. That means the remaining box at the bottom left must be 2. A 2 can't be used to make 11, as the 9 is already in use. Use the 5 and the 6 to get to 11. Enter the 2 into its box.

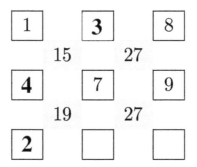

Solve the 19 sum by entering 6 into the bottom-middle box, as that's 19 - (2 + 7 + 4). That leaves 5 as the final digit for you to enter, and you've completed the puzzle.

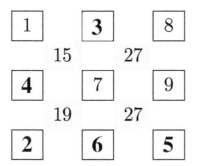

Breaking down the sums into their components is key to solving digit sum puzzles. That advice applies whether you're given more clues, as in this example, or fewer, as in some of the puzzles that follow. I prefer sparser puzzles. I think they're a little more fun with a better crunch.

With few clues to work with, use more logic. You might make more guesses, and might need to backtrack a few times. The underlying math is the same. You always have "this much left" in your sum and need to combine digits to reach your target number.

Background

For a time, I was under the impression that these puzzles were original to me. One rule of puzzles is that someone has usually thought it up before you. When writing this book, I found a short entry on Wikipedia about Sujiko puzzles.[6]

Sujiko was developed by Jai Gomer of Kobayaashi Studios. The layout isn't the same as mine—Sujiko puzzles use a mix of squares and circles—but the idea and rules seem identical. According to the write-up, they appear in UK newspapers. That may be why I hadn't encountered them.

I have built many puzzles. I'm not surprised to find other variations like this puzzle and the Zehnergitter puzzles from Puzzle 2, Summing Grids, on page 17.

---

6.   https://en.wikipedia.org/wiki/Sujiko

Having Fun with More Puzzles

In the next few pages you'll find puzzles that vary in their number of clues and the layout. Not every puzzle starts with a clump of three. Enjoy them! An answer key follows the puzzles.

Puzzle 1

Puzzle 2

Puzzle 3

Puzzle 4

☐	5	☐
21	22	
1	6	☐
17	15	
☐	☐	☐

Puzzle 5

☐	☐	9
17	24	
☐	2	6
14	13	
☐	☐	☐

Puzzle 6

9	☐	☐
19	20	
☐	1	8
15	18	
☐	☐	☐

Puzzle 7

☐	☐	☐
16	26	
☐	2	7
15	20	
☐	☐	5

Puzzle 8

☐	9	☐
15	25	
☐	2	8
16	22	
☐	☐	☐

Puzzle 9

5	☐	☐
12	21	
☐	1	☐
17	19	
☐	☐	3

Puzzle 10

☐	☐	☐
24	24	
☐	7	5
25	17	
☐	☐	☐

Puzzle 11

☐	☐	☐
17	19	
☐	7	☐
22	25	
☐	4	☐

Puzzle 12

☐	☐	5
18	18	
☐	2	☐
13	20	
☐	☐	☐

Puzzle 13

☐	☐	☐
18	20	
☐	2	☐
11	22	
☐	☐	☐

Puzzle 14

☐	☐	☐
21	20	
☐	2	☐
18	18	
☐	☐	☐

Puzzle 15

☐	☐	☐
13	17	
☐	☐	☐
17	23	
☐	☐	☐

Puzzle 16

16   23

20   18

Solutions

Some puzzles may allow multiple answers, mostly due to reflection or rotation. This section contains a single answer for each puzzle. Some correct solutions may not exactly match this answer key. If the math is right, congratulations! It doesn't matter whether our answers agree.

Puzzle 1

9		3		7
21		22		
1		8		4
17		23		
2		6		5

Puzzle 2

4		7		1
28		19		
8		9		2
25		20		
5		3		6

Puzzle 3

5		7		6
22		16		
9		1		2
17		15		
3		4		8

Puzzle 4

9		5		7
21		22		
1		6		4
17		15		
8		2		3

Puzzle 5

5		7		9
17		24		
3		2		6
14		13		
8		1		4

Puzzle 6

9		6		5
19		20		
3		1		8
15		18		
4		7		2

Puzzle 7

1		9		8
	16		26	
4		2		7
	15		20	
3		6		5

Puzzle 8

1		9		6
	15		25	
3		2		8
	16		22	
4		7		5

Puzzle 9

5		4		7
	12		21	
2		1		9
	17		19	
8		6		3

Puzzle 10

2		9		3
	24		24	
6		7		5
	25		17	
8		4		1

Puzzle 11

5		3		1
	17		19	
2		7		8
	22		25	
9		4		6

Puzzle 12

7		8		5
	18		18	
1		2		3
	13		20	
4		6		9

Puzzle 13

7		4		6
	18		20	
5		2		8
	11		22	
1		3		9

Puzzle 14

4		9		1
	21		20	
6		2		8
	18		18	
7		3		5

Puzzle 15

7		3		4
	13		17	
2		1		9
	17		23	
6		8		5

Puzzle 16

4		1		9
	16		23	
6		5		8
	20		18	
7		2		3

Mathsticks

How to Play

 Here's an equation made with Roman numerals and matchsticks. The equation is incorrect. Fix it by moving just one match stick without laying a stick over the equal sign to make an inequality, ≠.

For more information about this puzzle and its solution, turn the page. When you're ready for more puzzles like this one, see Having Fun with More Puzzles, on page 147.

About This Puzzle

In ancient times, back when I was young and dinosaurs still roamed the earth, kids' menus and crayons were a rarity. Sitting in restaurants, we played with the odd things found in such places. These were mostly sticks and coasters, plus the occasional lemon wedge. The lemon wedge games ended poorly, often due to the unceasing cruelty of my sisters. I'll spare you those details.

So many restaurant coasters are now round and flimsy. They've lost the architectural possibilities of multistory buildings we carefully built back then. As they had enough heft, you could also play a version of tiddlywinks with them. But you probably don't know what tiddlywinks is. Think "quarters" without the coins, the red cups, and with much angrier parents.

As for sticks, we played with a mix of them. We used wooden matchsticks, as people smoked back then. Even on airplanes! There were toothpicks, some frilly, some not, some with tiny umbrellas. Steak markers were flat and wooden. They let people know whose Salisbury steak was rare, as rare meat in restaurants was also a thing of that time.

Adults, attempting to drink and smoke and socialize, would try to get us kids to stop being children. This was not a possibility, of course, even if you were willing to go to jail or to wait long enough for dinner to arrive. Being ever hopeful, though, they would sometimes create little puzzles from sticks. Some puzzles made you rearrange squares and triangles. Others were word puzzles. Depending on the adult, we often saw the same puzzles over and over. In return, we astonished them with our well-practiced "genius."

Every now and then, an adult pulled out a Roman numeral matchstick puzzle. Instead of, for example, turning four triangles into six, you could move a single matchstick and fix an equation. They were so much fun. I was hooked for life.

I wish I had some sort of story to tell about ancient matchstick games. How similar games were played in medieval Japan. Sadly, I don't. For one thing, I don't know where these fix-the-math stick puzzles come from. Also, I'm pretty sure Roman numerals were pretty local to Europe. In preparing this book, I couldn't track down a history, which is why I'm telling you about my demented sisters and the world-ending evil they committed with lemon wedges instead. There doesn't seem to be a definitive "Art of the Roman Matchstick Math Puzzle" to reference. And yet, I remember playing matchstick games from the time I was small. They're still popular.

I've played several variations. Some have you add a stick, others remove one. The ones I like the best have you move a single stick to correct an incorrect equation. Your job is to fix the equation and restore an equality with that single change.

Solving the Example

This sample equation doesn't work because four minus two is two, not seven. Moving the I from the IV onto the minus sign fixes this problem. The equation is now balanced and correct. Five plus two is, indeed, seven.

$$V + II = VII$$

Solving Puzzles

There are many Roman numeral puzzles to solve. Changes are limited: for each symbol in your equation, you can add or remove a stick. Or you can move a stick to a new position, or "mutate" by adjusting a stick ever so slightly.

The chart on page 146 shows the ways you can affect numbers. I made this chart to help me design my puzzles. It's not exhaustive, stopping at 20, which I felt was fine for my needs. The chart shows you all the ways different Roman numerals relate to each other, providing the source for the puzzles in this chapter.

The parentheses in the chart are transformations that are a little iffy. It can be hard to make nineteen (XIX) into twenty (XX). It may leave too much space between the two Xs. Changing XVI into XIV needs space for that extra I to fit. When laying out puzzles, make sure the spaces work.

In addition to numbers, there are the three math symbols: plus, minus, and equal. All of these can be transformed into each other by removing, moving, or adding a stick.

Symbol	Add	Remove	Move	Mutate
I	II, +			-
II	III	I		+
III		II		
IV		V	VI	IX
V	IV, VI			X
VI	VII	V	IV	XI
VII	VIII	VI		XII
VIII		VII		XIII
IX		X	XI	IV
X	IX, XI			V
XI	XII	X	IX	VI
XII	XIII	XI		VII
XIII		XII		VIII
XIV		(XV)	(XVI)	XIX
XV	XVI, (XIV)		(XIV)	XX
XVI	XVII	XV	(XIV)	XXI
XVII	XVIII	XVI		XXII
XVIII		XVII		XXIII
XIX		(XX)	(XXI)	XIV
XX	XXI (XIX)			XV

Having Fun with More Puzzles

You've seen a walk-through and viewed a puzzle design chart. Are you ready to give some actual puzzles a try? Get ready to move matchsticks—but just one per puzzle!

Puzzle 1

$$IX + V = III$$

Puzzle 2

$$X - V = X$$

Puzzle 3

$$III - II = IV$$

Puzzle 4

$$V + II = XII$$

Puzzle 5

$$X - I = XI$$

Puzzle 6

$$XII + V = VI$$

Puzzle 7

$$|| + | = |$$

$$V| - |V = |X$$

Puzzle 9

$$|| + V = X||$$

$$V + || = |V$$

Puzzle 11

$$|V = |V - |$$

$$X| - XX = |X$$

Puzzle 13

$$X||| = |V + |V$$

Puzzle 14

$$XII - V = II$$

Puzzle 15

$$I - III = II$$

Puzzle 16

$$VI + II = V$$

Puzzle 17

$$VII + V = X$$

Puzzle 18

$$I \ X \ III = VII$$

Puzzle 19

$$II + V = V$$

Puzzle 20

$$V = III - II$$

Puzzle 21

$$VI - I = VI$$

Puzzle 22

$$III + I = I$$

Puzzle 23

$$XX + I = XIX$$

Puzzle 24

$$IX + I = XII$$

Puzzle 25

$$XI - XX = IX$$

Puzzle 26

$$I - II = II$$

Puzzle 27

$$VIII + I = XI$$

Puzzle 28

$$XI + I = X$$

Solutions

Many of these puzzles have multiple answers. These are the ways I designed and solved them. Your answer may differ.

Puzzle 1	Puzzle 2
Original: IX + V = III	*Original*: X - V = X
Move the vertical bar in the + after the V. The equation now reads: IX - VI = III	Pull the / on the rightmost X to the right to convert the X into a V. The corrected equation: X - V = V

Puzzle 3	Puzzle 4
Original: III - II = IV	*Original*: V + II = XII
Move the rightmost I from the III onto the minus sign. Now the equation is: II + II = IV	To correct this equation, convert the X into a V by pulling the \ stick to the left: V + II = VII

Puzzle 5	Puzzle 6
Original: X - I = XI	*Original*: XII + V = VI
Move the I from XI on the right of the equation to the X on the left. The math is now: XI - I = X	Move the vertical bar from the plus, changing it into a minus sign. Add that matchstick after the VI, making it a VII: XII - V = VII

Puzzle 7	Puzzle 8
Original: II + I = I	*Original*: VI - IV = IX
Move the leftmost I to the right of the equation: I + I = II	Move the I in VI onto the minus sign, converting it to a plus: V + IV = IX

Puzzle 9	Puzzle 10
Original: II + V = XII	*Original*: V + II = IV
Drag the \ in V onto /, converting the V into a X:	Move the vertical line in the plus sign after the first V, to make a VI:
II + X = XII	VI - II = IV

Puzzle 11	Puzzle 12
Original: IV = IV - I	*Original*: XI - XX = IX
Move the I in the first IV onto the minus sign to use addition:	Move the top matchstick from the equal sign to above the minus sign to reverse the two symbols:
V = IV + I	XI = XX - IX

Puzzle 13	Puzzle 14
Original: XIII = IV + IV	*Original*: XII - V = II
Move the \ on either IV to convert the V to an X:	Convert the X into a V by dragging the \ to the left:
XIII = IX + IV	VII - V = II

Puzzle 15	Puzzle 16
Original: I - III = II	*Original*: VI + II = V
Move the top matchstick from the equal sign to above the minus sign. This reverses these two symbols:	Move the vertical from the plus sign to before the V, creating a IV:
	VI - II = IV
I = III - II	

Puzzle 17	Puzzle 18
Original: VII + V = X	*Original*: I X III = VII
Move the second I from VII to after the X:	This is the one time I played with "X" as a multiplication symbol. Convert the I to a minus sign by rotating it sideways. Then place it between the X and the III, converting "X" to ten:
VI + V = XI	X - III = VII
	Alternately, move the final I from the VII to the I at the start:
	II X III = VI

Puzzle 19	Puzzle 20
Original: II + V = V	*Original*: V = III - II
Move an I from the II to after the final V:	Move the top line from the equal sign to the minus, swapping the two symbols:
I + V = VI	V - III = II

Puzzle 21	Puzzle 22
Original: VI - I = VI	*Original*: III + I = I
Move the I from VI to the minus sign, changing it to a plus:	Move the upright from the plus to the right of the equation:
V + I = VI	III - I = II

Puzzle 23	Puzzle 24
Original: XX + I = XIX	*Original*: IX + I = XII
Move the I from within XIX to after the second X:	Move the rightmost I in XII to the I, making the two numbers II and XI:
XX + I = XXI	IX + II = XI

Puzzle 25	Puzzle 26
Original: XI - XX = IX	*Original*: I - II = II
Move the top line from the equal sign to the minus sign, swapping the two symbols:	Move a I from the first II onto the minus sign:
XI = XX - IX	I + I = II

Puzzle 27	Puzzle 28
Original: VIII + I = XI	*Original*: XI + I = X
Move the I in the XI from the right to the left, making IX:	Move the I in XI to the X on the right:
VIII + I = IX	X + I = XI

Bit Puzzles

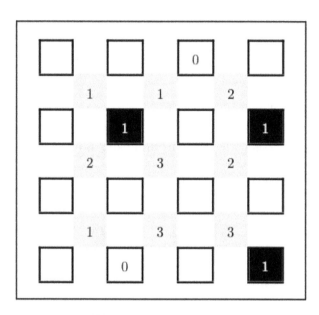

How to Play

 Enter 1 or 0 into each empty square such that the sum of each group of four squares is the number shown between them.

For more information about this puzzle and its solution, turn the page. When you're ready for more puzzles like this one, see Having Fun with More Puzzles, on page 160.

About This Puzzle

Bit puzzles are simple, but I think they're a lot of fun. They're named after the computer bit, which can store a one or a zero. The board includes grey hints and white squares. Enter 1 or 0 into each empty square, filling the grid.

A hint sits between each group of four squares. It shows the sum of those squares. If the hint is 2, for example, then two squares have 1s in them and the others are 0. Use logic and math to reason through the hidden pattern and fill every square.

Solving the Example

As with any puzzle, look for places where you can break into the grid. In this example, there's a pre-filled 1 toward the top-left corner. That resolves the two sums above it. Enter the zeros around each sum.

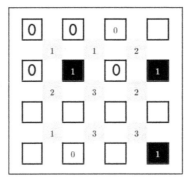

With those filled, you can resolve the sum of 2 at the top right and 3 in the middle. Enter the missing 1s, and the board is getting close to completion.

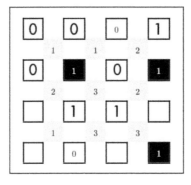

You now have the information you need to complete the grid. Enter 0s on the third row, and a 0 and 1 on the fourth.

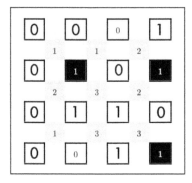

This was a quick solve. The board was small. There were clues pre-filled on your behalf. Bit puzzles become more challenging as the board grows and clues decrease.

Background

Bit puzzles are one of my favorite time-wasters these days. I like their simplicity. I find the logic strategies soothing. As far as I know, they are original. So, you know, all rights reserved and all. Similar puzzles may be out there. I have not seen them, but math is math.

Like the name, I envisioned the puzzles as computer bits, ones and zeros, either on or off. My pre-filled clues are either filled in with black or empty on white on the page to reflect that. This gives a visual punch to the on-off style.

You'll find two variations in the following puzzles: the gray sums, as in the just-worked example, and hints relating to the number 2 in other puzzles. Sums can equal 2, exceed 2 (3 or 4), or be less than 2 (0 or 1). With slightly less information, they're a little more challenging. I like both styles. I hope you do too.

As in other chapters, these puzzles progress from easy to harder. I prefer bigger boards with just a few clues. I've added a couple of large puzzles to the end. They're fast and fun even at the larger sizes.

Having Fun with More Puzzles

Depending on the layout, puzzle answers are not always unique.

Puzzle 1

Puzzle 2

Puzzle 3

Puzzle 4

Puzzle 5

Puzzle 6

2	1	0	1	
1	0			
3	3	2	1	
1	2	2	2	
0				

Puzzle 7

	1			0
3	3	2	1	
1	1			0
4	2	1	2	
3	3	2	3	

Puzzle 8

			1	
< 2	= 2	= 2	< 2	
1				
= 2	= 2	= 2	< 2	
1				
> 2	= 2	= 2	< 2	
1				

Puzzle 9

Puzzle 10

Puzzle 11

Puzzle 12

Puzzle 13

Puzzle 14

Puzzle 15

Puzzle 16

Solutions

Keep in mind that some bit puzzles have multiple solutions.

Puzzle 1

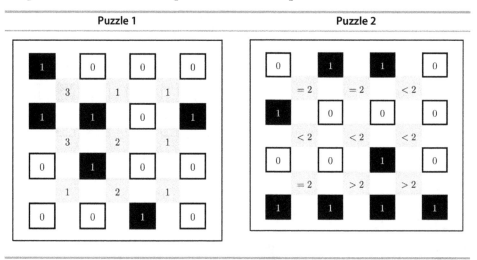

Puzzle 2

Puzzle 3

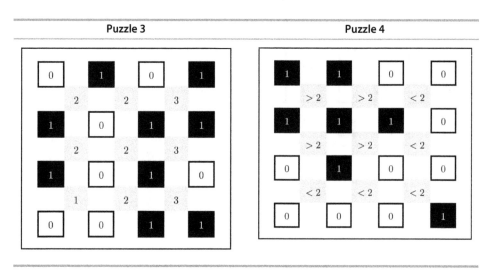

Puzzle 4

Puzzle 5

```
0   1   0   1   0
  2   3   3   3
0   1   1   1   1
  1   3   3   3
0   0   1   0   1
  1   2   2   1
1   0   1   0   0
```

Puzzle 6

```
0   0   0   0   1
  2   1   0   1
1   1   0   0   0
  3   3   2   1
0   1   1   1   0
  1   2   2   2
0   0   0   0   1
```

Puzzle 7

```
0   1   1   0   0
  3   3   2   1
1   1   0   1   0
  4   2   1   2
1   1   0   0   1
  3   3   2   3
0   1   1   1   1
```

Puzzle 8

```
0    0    1    1    0
  <2   =2   =2   <2
0    1    0    0    0
  =2   =2   =2   <2
1    0    1    1    0
  >2   =2   =2   <2
1    1    0    0    0
```

Puzzle 9

```
0   1   1   0   1
  2   3   2   2
0   1   0   1   0
  2   2   1   2
0   1   0   0   1
  2   1   1   3
1   0   0   1   1
```

Puzzle 10

```
1   1   1   1   1
  4   3   2   2
1   1   0   0   0
  2   1   1   2
0   0   0   1   1
  1   1   2   3
1   0   1   0   1
```

Puzzle 11

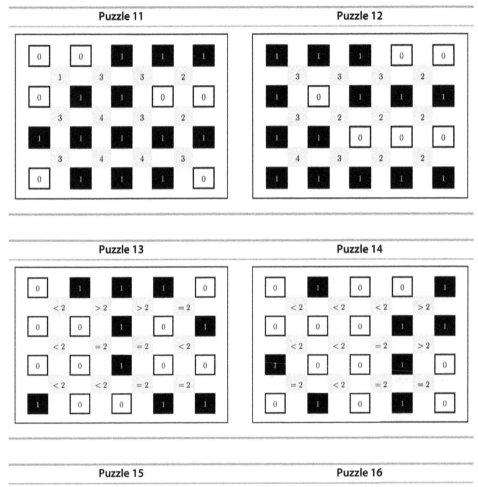

Puzzle 12

Puzzle 13

Puzzle 14

Puzzle 15

Puzzle 16

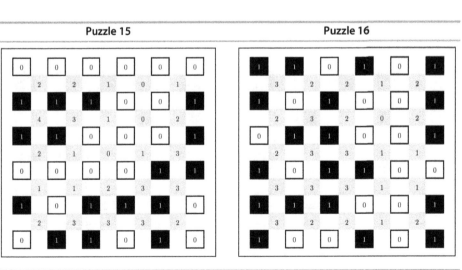

Index

Thank you!

We hope you enjoyed this book and that you're already thinking about what you want to learn next. To help make that decision easier, we're offering you this gift.

Head on over to https://pragprog.com right now, and use the coupon code BUYANOTHER2023 to save 30% on your next ebook. Offer is void where prohibited or restricted. This offer does not apply to any edition of the *The Pragmatic Programmer* ebook.

And if you'd like to share your own expertise with the world, why not propose a writing idea to us? After all, many of our best authors started off as our readers, just like you. With a 50% royalty, world-class editorial services, and a name you trust, there's nothing to lose. Visit https://pragprog.com/become-an-author/ today to learn more and to get started.

We thank you for your continued support, and we hope to hear from you again soon!

The Pragmatic Bookshelf

SAVE 30%!
Use coupon code
BUYANOTHER2023

Rust Brain Teasers

The Rust programming language is consistent and does its best to avoid surprising the programmer. Like all languages, though, Rust still has its quirks. But these quirks present a teaching opportunity. In this book, you'll work through a series of brain teasers that will challenge your understanding of Rust. By understanding the gaps in your knowledge, you can become better at what you do and avoid mistakes. Many of the teasers in this book come from the author's own experience creating software. Others derive from commonly asked questions in the Rust community. Regardless of their origin, these brain teasers are fun, and let's face it: who doesn't love a good puzzle, right?

Herbert Wolverson
(138 pages) ISBN: 9781680509175. $18.95
https://pragprog.com/book/hwrustbrain

Pandas Brain Teasers

This book contains 25 short programs that will challenge your understanding of Pandas. Like any big project, the Pandas developers had to make some design decisions that at times seem surprising. This book uses those quirks as a teaching opportunity. By understanding the gaps in your knowledge, you'll become better at what you do. Some of the teasers are from the author's experience shipping bugs to production, and some from others doing the same. Teasers and puzzles are fun, and learning how to solve them can teach you to avoid programming mistakes and maybe even impress your colleagues and future employers.

Miki Tebeka
(110 pages) ISBN: 9781680509014. $18.95
https://pragprog.com/book/d-pandas

Go Brain Teasers

This book contains 25 short programs that will challenge your understanding of Go. Like any big project, the Go developers had to make some design decisions that at times seem surprising. This book uses those quirks as a teaching opportunity. By understanding the gaps in your knowledge, you'll become better at what you do. Some of the teasers are from the author's experience shipping bugs to production, and some from others doing the same. Teasers and puzzles are fun, and learning how to solve them can teach you to avoid programming mistakes and maybe even impress your colleagues and future employers.

Miki Tebeka
(110 pages) ISBN: 9781680508994. $18.95
https://pragprog.com/book/d-gobrain

Python Brain Teasers

We geeks love puzzles and solving them. The Python programming language is a simple one, but like all other languages it has quirks. This book uses those quirks as teaching opportunities via 30 simple Python programs that challenge your understanding of Python. The teasers will help you avoid mistakes, see gaps in your knowledge, and become better at what you do. Use these teasers to impress your co-workers or just to pass the time in those boring meetings. Teasers are fun!

Miki Tebeka
(116 pages) ISBN: 9781680509007. $18.95
https://pragprog.com/book/d-pybrain

Mazes for Programmers

A book on mazes? Seriously?

Yes!

Not because you spend your day creating mazes, or because you particularly like solving mazes.

But because it's fun. Remember when programming used to be fun? This book takes you back to those days when you were starting to program, and you wanted to make your code do things, draw things, and solve puzzles. It's fun because it lets you explore and grow your code, and reminds you how it feels to just think.

Sometimes it feels like you live your life in a maze of twisty little passages, all alike. Now you can code your way out.

Jamis Buck
(286 pages) ISBN: 9781680500554. $38
https://pragprog.com/book/jbmaze

Good Math

Mathematics is beautiful—and it can be fun and exciting as well as practical. *Good Math* is your guide to some of the most intriguing topics from two thousand years of mathematics: from Egyptian fractions to Turing machines; from the real meaning of numbers to proof trees, group symmetry, and mechanical computation. If you've ever wondered what lay beyond the proofs you struggled to complete in high school geometry, or what limits the capabilities of the computer on your desk, this is the book for you.

Mark C. Chu-Carroll
(282 pages) ISBN: 9781937785338. $34
https://pragprog.com/book/mcmath

Exercises for Programmers

When you write software, you need to be at the top of your game. Great programmers practice to keep their skills sharp. Get sharp and stay sharp with more than fifty practice exercises rooted in real-world scenarios. If you're a new programmer, these challenges will help you learn what you need to break into the field, and if you're a seasoned pro, you can use these exercises to learn that hot new language for your next gig.

Brian P. Hogan
(118 pages) ISBN: 9781680501223. $24
https://pragprog.com/book/bhwb

Practical Programming, Third Edition

Classroom-tested by tens of thousands of students, this new edition of the best-selling intro to programming book is for anyone who wants to understand computer science. Learn about design, algorithms, testing, and debugging. Discover the fundamentals of programming with Python 3.6—a language that's used in millions of devices. Write programs to solve real-world problems, and come away with everything you need to produce quality code. This edition has been updated to use the new language features in Python 3.6.

Paul Gries, Jennifer Campbell, Jason Montojo
(410 pages) ISBN: 9781680502688. $49.95
https://pragprog.com/book/gwpy3

The Pragmatic Bookshelf

The Pragmatic Bookshelf features books written by professional developers for professional developers. The titles continue the well-known Pragmatic Programmer style and continue to garner awards and rave reviews. As development gets more and more difficult, the Pragmatic Programmers will be there with more titles and products to help you stay on top of your game.

Visit Us Online

This Book's Home Page
https://pragprog.com/book/esbrain
Source code from this book, errata, and other resources. Come give us feedback, too!

Keep Up-to-Date
https://pragprog.com
Join our announcement mailing list (low volume) or follow us on Twitter @pragprog for new titles, sales, coupons, hot tips, and more.

New and Noteworthy
https://pragprog.com/news
Check out the latest Pragmatic developments, new titles, and other offerings.

Save on the ebook

Save on the ebook versions of this title. Owning the paper version of this book entitles you to purchase the electronic versions at a terrific discount.

PDFs are great for carrying around on your laptop—they are hyperlinked, have color, and are fully searchable. Most titles are also available for the iPhone and iPod touch, Amazon Kindle, and other popular e-book readers.

Send a copy of your receipt to support@pragprog.com and we'll provide you with a discount coupon.

Contact Us

Online Orders:	*https://pragprog.com/catalog*
Customer Service:	*support@pragprog.com*
International Rights:	*translations@pragprog.com*
Academic Use:	*academic@pragprog.com*
Write for Us:	*http://write-for-us.pragprog.com*
Or Call:	+1 800-699-7764

Lightning Source UK Ltd.
Milton Keynes UK
UKHW030627050123
414831UK00001B/1